I0132150

William Sharp, Philip Bourke Marston

Poems and Lyrics of Love's Joy and Sorrow

William Sharp, Philip Bourke Marston

Poems and Lyrics of Love's Joy and Sorrow

ISBN/EAN: 9783744712316

Printed in Europe, USA, Canada, Australia, Japan

Cover: Foto ©Thomas Meinert / pixelio.de

More available books at **www.hansebooks.com**

SONG-TIDE: POEMS AND LYRICS OF LOVE'S JOY AND SORROW. BY PHILIP BOURKE MARSTON. EDITED, WITH INTRODUCTORY MEMOIR, BY WILLIAM SHARP.

LONDON
WALTER SCOTT, 24 WARWICK LANE
PATERNOSTER ROW
1888

NOTE.

The main title of this volume is identical with that of Philip Bourke Marston's first book. The poems are selected from *Song-Tide* and from *Wind-Voices*, both out of print, and (by the courtesy of Messrs. Chatto & Windus) from *All in All.* The *Garden Secrets* are, with one addition, printed from the little volume bearing that title, and issued last Christmas in America by Messrs. Roberts Bros., edited by Mrs. Louise Chandler Moulton.

DEDICATED

TO

WESTLAND MARSTON, LL.D.,

POET AND DRAMATIST,

THE FATHER, COMPANION, AND FRIEND

OF

"THE BLIND POET,"

P. B. M.

CONTENTS.

POEMS FROM "ALL IN ALL"—

SONNETS FROM "SONG-TIDE"—

SONNETS FROM "SONG-TIDE"—*continued.*

SONNETS FROM "ALL IN ALL"

GARDEN SECRETS—

POEMS AND BALLADS FROM "WIND-VOICES"—

POEMS AND BALLADS FROM "WIND-VOICES"—*continued*

OF LOVE: ELEVEN LYRICS—

TO PHILIP BOURKE MARSTON,

INCITING ME TO POETIC WORK.

Sweet Poet, thou of whom these years that roll
  Must one day yet the burdened birthright learn,
  And by the darkness of thine eyes discern
How piercing was the sight within thy soul;—
Gifted apart, thou goest to the great goal,
  A cloud-bound radiant spirit, strong to earn,
  Light-reft, that prize for which fond myriads yearn
Vainly light-blest,—the Seër's aureole.

And doth thine ear, divinely dowered to catch
  All spheral sounds in thy song blent so well,
  Still hearken for my voice's slumbering spell
With wistful love? Ah! let the muse now snatch
My wreath for thy young brows, and bend to watch
  Thy veiled transfiguring sense's miracle.

DANTE GABRIEL ROSSETTI.

MEMOIR

OF

PHILIP BOURKE MARSTON.

"IN this life calamity follows calamity by no apparent law of cause and effect. In the web that destiny spins there is a terrible and a cruel symmetry, which no theory of 'circumstance' can explain. When once the pattern of their tapestry is sombre, the Fates never leave it incomplete." To no one could these words by the author of "Aylwin" be more applicable than to Philip Bourke Marston, whose death more than a year ago enfranchised him from long suffering, brought him that surcease for which he had yearned with an ever-deepening intensity. He dwelt continually in the shadow of a great gloom, for in addition to the physical affliction which in the most literal sense darkened his life, the evil mischances of Fate sorely wrought against him. "If one were not too insignificant for the metaphor," he once remarked, "I could with bitter truth assert that the stars in their courses have ever fought against me." It has not been the lot of many men of letters to experience so much sorrow with such little alloy of the common pleasures of life. Those who are most cruelly afflicted are generally the least querulous, the least noisily resentful ; hence the misapprehension of some among the casual acquaintances of "the blind poet" who believed that Marston's compensations must have been numerous to have enabled him to bear the brave front before the world which was his characteristic attitude. But till fatal illness overcame him he could laugh with or take keen interest in the affairs of a friend, as if for him life had but the same significance as for the majority of men.

Philip Bourke Marston was the third child and only son of the well-known dramatist and poet, Dr. Westland Marston. His mother was a woman of as great charm of mind as of body, and endeared herself to her son by her penetrative sympathy and tenderness. Philip was born in London on the 13th of August, in the year 1850 ; his second baptismal name, Bourke, was that of a family connection, and "Philip" was prefixed to it out of Dr. Marston's affectionate regard for his friend, Philip James Bailey, the author of *Festus.* Miss Dinah Mulock (Mrs. Craik) became godmother to the little boy, and it was for him that the popular authoress of *John Halifax, Gentleman* wrote the now familiar lyric, entitled "Philip, my King." An unconscious prophecy, to be only too adequately realised, was uttered in one of the stanzas of this poem—

"One day,
Philip, my king,
Thou too must tread, as we trod, a way
Thorny and cruel and cold and grey."

Philip had two sisters; the elder, Eleanor (Nellie), who afterwards became the wife of Arthur O'Shaughnessy, author of *The Epic of Women* and of other volumes of poetry; and the younger, Cicely, who throughout his youth was to prove to him a second self. While in his fourth year, his sister Nellie was prostrated by scarlatina, and in order to render Philip as secure as practicable from the insidious disease he was given quantities of belladonna, probably an excellent remedy, but one which proved over-potent in the case of Dr. Marston's delicate and sensitive little boy. The eyes are supposed to have suffered from the action of the medicine ; but further, and probably more irremediable, harm was endured by a blow which the child received during play with some boisterous companions. Inflammation set in, first in one eye and then in the other ; and ere long incipient cataract became only too obvious. At this time the boy's beauty was remarkable. I remember Mrs. Craik's stating that she had never seen a lovelier child—an assertion corroborated by others who knew Philip in his infancy. Lady Hardy has told me how she was perplexed by the way in which he was wont to run up against chairs and tables, as if he had miscalculated their distances—though he was quite of an age to have estimated these aright. It was soon after this that his sight became more seriously affected. Some years later an operation was performed, and a measure of temporary relief was thus afforded ; but as time lapsed there could be no further doubt that a doom of blindness was inevitable. The best oculists were consulted, and everything that loving anxiety suggested was done. But all was without avail, and as the months went past even Mrs. Marston surrendered her long lingering hopes.

Marston's mental powers began to exert themselves at a very early period, although of necessity his opportunities towards intellectual development were sadly modified by his blindness. As it was, he produced while yet in his teens some distinctly noteworthy poetry. Poems such as "A Christmas Vigil," lyrics like "The Rose and the Wind," do not read as if they were immature efforts. The latter is perhaps unsurpassed by any lyrical poem in our modern literature written in an author's nonage. Marston was not then wholly blind—that is to say, he not only easily distinguished night from day, and even sunshine from cloud-gloom, but could discern the difference between men and women by their relative sizes and the shape of their garments: the morning, during his boyhood and early youth, was not wholly deprived of its beauty, and moonlight evenings were a source of infinite solace and delight. For the sea he early conceived a passion. It afforded him an ecstasy of enjoyment—wherein pain almost as largely prevailed as pleasure—and, taking his blindness into account, there have been few more daring swimmers. He would listen to the roar upon the beach, or to the strange rhythmical tumult of the seaward waves, innumerably marching in vast battalions, or to the murmur of the surge where the sea slept against the sand, with an expression so rapt, that for the time his soul seemed to look through his shadowed eyes and to animate his face with the glow of its presence. If throughout his weary latter years he yearned for anything more than for death, it was for the neighbourhood of the sea—its ultimate silence to be about him, its moving music to be his requiem. And thus it was that his most treasured reminiscences were of broad spaces of moonlight and of the deep lustrous green of sea-water.

To a dear friend, Mrs. Moulton, he once energetically stated, "No! I was *not* blind, then. I couldn't read, of course, or see the faces of people; but I could see the tree-boughs waving in the wind, and I could see the pageant of sunset in the west, and the glimmer of a fire upon the hearth, and oh, it was such a different thing from the days that came afterwards, when I could not see anything!"

Philip Marston's first and not least loving amanuensis was his mother, who not only wrote out for her blind boy his early attempts in prose and verse, but also acted delicately and wisely the part of critic. To her love he owed much, nor was he ever chary of acknowledgment of his indebtedness. But partly as cares accumulated upon Mrs. Marston, thus preventing her from such ceaseless devotion to her son as she would fain have given, and partly from purely natural reasons, Philip's closest companion was his sister Cicely, who may without exaggeration be said to have devoted her whole life to her brother. A tribute to her ceaseless sympathy and love was given by the latter in the stanzas inscribed to Cicely Narney Marston,* two of which I may here appropriately quote.

"Oh, in what things have we not been as one?
Oh, more than any sister ever was
To any brother! Ere my days be done,
And this my little strength of singing pass,
I would these failing lines of mine might show
All thou hast been, as well as all thou art.
And yet what need? for all who meet thee know
Thy queenliness of intellect and heart.

"Oh, dear companion in the land of thought,
How often hast thou led me by thy voice
Through paths where men not all in vain have sought
For consolation, when their cherished joys
Lie dead before them . . . .
. . . .
Thy love to me is as thy precious hand
Might be upon my forehead if it burned
In hell, of some last fever: hold me fast,
Oh thou to whom in joy's full noon I turned,
As now I turn, the glory being past."

If it had not been for his blindness, Philip Marston's youth would have been fortunate beyond comparison with that of almost any other young poet of whom there is record. Dr. Westland Marston was not only a successful dramatist, but

* (*See page* 81 *hereafter.*)

one of the most popular literary men in London. There were few houses where were frequent *réunions* more enjoyable than those in the villa near Chalk Farm. There, occasionally, would be Dante Gabriel Rossetti and his brother William, Dr. Gordon Hake, William Morris, Swinburne, and many other celebrities and "coming men." Philip turned as naturally towards those benign intellectual influences as the heliotrope to the sun: his poetic development was rapid, and before he had emerged from his teens he had written—as has already been stated—some eminently noteworthy poetry.

While yet under twenty-one, Philip Marston loved a beautiful girl, Miss Mary Nesbit. The passion of the young poet was returned, and—notwithstanding the darkness in which he dwelt—a life of beauty and even joy opened up before the ardent youth. Affectionate and indulgent parents, a self-sacrificing and adoring sister, the love of a beautiful girl, congenial society, and brilliant literary prospects—each and all of these made up a lot which, if the fulfilment had equalled the promise, would have banished the gloom from Philip's life. The shadow of melancholy that haunts the poetic soul, and perhaps a constitutional tendency to excess of emotion, combined with darkened sight, account for the sad and occasionally sombre tone which characterises many of the sonnets and shorter poems written during this halcyon period.

While he was putting together the poems which were to make up his first volume (a few of which, it may be mentioned here, had already appeared in the *Cornhill* and other magazines) his mother was prostrated by what proved to be a fatal illness. All who knew Mrs. Marston loved her, but to no one was her loss a greater blow than to that son whom she had so lovingly tended, to whom she had been as a friend as well as a mother. His grief was intense, and more than ever he writhed under the curse of his affliction; if only, he yearningly cried, he could have one ever-to-be-remembered glimpse of the beloved dead who had been to him so much of his light of life.

But the elasticity of youth and the quick succession of new and vivid interests overcame the extremity of his sorrow, and he began to look forward to years of comparative happiness and prosperity.

It was about this time that he won the love of Miss Nesbit. Perhaps if his eyes had not been dimmed he would have foreseen the shadow of a new and irremediable disaster. Miss Nesbit was far from robust, but only a few friends knew that she had developed symptoms of consumption. She bore her unseen crown of sorrow bravely, and only when it became certain that her life was no longer secure for any length of time did she endeavour to warn her lover of the inevitable. But love had blinded his inner vision, and he either did not realise or else refused to allow himself to believe what was with infinite gentleness hinted to him.

Before I pass away from the record of his youth —for with the next and most terrible calamity he became old beyond the warrant of his years—I may quote a few passages from an obituary notice by one of Marston's most intimate and most loyal friends, Mrs. Louise Chandler Moulton, the well-known American poet and romancist, prefixing to these passages an excerpt describing her first meeting with the young poet when in his twenty-sixth year.

"I first met him," writes Mrs. Moulton, "at a literary evening—a sort of authors' night—at a well-known London house, and I knew the blind poet would be among the guests—the one, indeed, whom I felt most interest in meeting. I soon perceived him, standing beside his sister Cicely—a slight, rather tall man of twenty-six, very young-looking even for his age. He had a wonderfully fine brow. His brown eyes were still beautiful in shape and colour. His dark-brown hair and beard had glints of chestnut; and all his colouring was rich and warm. His was a singularly refined face, with a beautiful expression when in repose—keenly sensitive, but with full, pleasure-loving lips, that made one understand how hard his limitations must be for him to whom beauty and pleasure were so dear. At that time the colour came and went in his cheeks as in those of a sensitive girl. . . . How many tales he has told me of his darkened, dream-haunted childhood! He began very early to feel the full pain of his loss of vision. He fell in love, when he was not more than ten years old, with a beautiful young lady, and went through all a lover's gamut of joys and pains; and sometimes the torture of not being able to behold the beauty of his adored was so extreme that he used to dash his head against the wall in a sudden mad longing to be done at once with life and sorrow. Yet the love of life was keen in him, and his earliest childhood was haunted by visions of future fame, which should make people acknowledge that though blind his soul yet saw unshared visions. His *life* was his education. His house was the resort of many of the intellectual giants of that time; and every day's guests were his unconscious teachers. He was fourteen, I think, when he first met Swinburne, who was just then the idol of his boyish worship. At that time —so wonderful was his memory—he actually knew by heart the whole of the first series of *Poems and Ballads*. He was taken to see his demi-god, and entered the sacred presence with a heart beating almost to suffocation; and went home feeling that his hopes and dreams had been, for once, fulfilled. To the very end of his days Swinburne's friendship was a pride and joy to him."

In 1871 a great event occurred. *Song-Tide*, the first-fruits of the young poet's genius, was published, and immediately received a warm and unmistakably genuine welcome. The leading literary journals hailed the advent of a new poet, and that cultivated section of the public which is ever alert for what new thing of promise may come to light, speculated with interest as to the possibilities of the new singer.

While there was still hope that Miss Nesbit might recover—and by this time the lover's heart was often sore beset with terrible forebodings—Philip Marston's heart was gladdened by the receipt of the first copy of the book over which he had long been lovingly engaged. In it he had enshrined his love in many a beautiful sonnet and lyric, and in the delight of placing the first copy in the hands of his betrothed he almost overlooked what to every one else was becoming too evident.

In the autumn of 1871 Miss Nesbit was spending a visit with some friends in Normandy, but the change wrought no benefit. Philip Marston was a guest in the same house. A very painful story concerning the circumstances of her death has gained currency, and has even appeared in one or two journals. This story, which asserts that the blind lover did not know of his betrothed's death, and, accidentally gaining access to her room unnoticed, ascertained the truth with a fearful suddenness and directness, is, so far as Dr. Westland Marston's knowledge goes, not the case. The bereaved young poet did indeed sit in a voiceless, tearless agony by the bedside of the girl whom he had so passionately loved, but it would seem that he had first learned the bitter news from lovingly sympathetic lips.

With this great sorrow the youth of Philip Marston died an early death. Simultaneously, darkness came upon the dimmed eyes; bitter tears, tears of many hopeless days and sleepless nights, of unavailing regret and vain yearning, quenched the flickering flame. Thenceforth a deep gloom prevailed throughout the remnant of his years. Verily, it seemed as if indeed, in his own words, "the gods derided him."

But even so supreme a loss, even such overwhelming calamities, cannot prevent human nature from finding relief in possible pleasures or partial diversions.

More and more Cicely devoted herself to her unhappy brother, alleviating much of his grief, endlessly helping, suggesting, amusing, and acting for him. She became to him almost a necessity of life ; without her he did not consider it possible he could endure the infinite weariness and sorrow which encompassed him.

Brother and sister went to live together in lodgings, firstly at Notting Hill and later in the Euston Road. They had sufficient means between them to enable them to live in fair comfort, and Marston was entering upon that sustained intellectual drudgery which brought him such bitterly inadequate monetary recompense, but which continually extended his sympathies and won for him new friends and admirers. Henceforth, except for an interval when Cicely stayed with the Madox Browns, the two lived together in their London lodgings, save when they went into the country or to the seaside, to France, and once to Italy. For certain golden weeks, a "sovereign season," Philip Marston revelled, sightless as he was, in the manifold delights of Italy ; Florence and Venice especially enthralled him, and throughout his life the memory of this happy time remained unsered. He was wont to speak of his experiences in a manner that puzzled new acquaintances. He would dwell longingly on the splendour of the view from Fiesole or Bellosguardo, of the glory of light and shade athwart the slopes of Vallombrosa, of the joyous aspects of Florence itself, of the transmuting glamour of the scirocco, of sunset and moonrise upon the Venetian lagunes. Still more would he puzzle people by such remarks as "I don't like So-and-so's appearance : he has a look on his face which I mistrust," or "London looks so sombre ; I like to see a place seeming as if it were aware of such things as sunlight and flowers." In this there was nothing of affectation, although it is undeniable that Marston was always very sensitive to any reference to his blindness : his sister Cicely had become his second sight. Through her he saw and understood, and had pleasure in those things which otherwise would have been for him more or less sealed mysteries.

After this happy experience—too short, alas ! and clouded with sad memories—Marston settled down to a regular literary life. His means, he used to say half-humorously, were children of Mercury : every note, every sovereign was winged, and departed from his possession with an expedition which was at once mysterious and alarming. In fact, then as always, his generosity and hospitality knew no limits. As these means gradually began to disappear, and as the struggle for existence became keener, his open-handedness knew no abatement, and to the end he practised the same liberality.

While never tired of the company of that well-loved sister, he naturally formed new and valued friendships. From first to last, however, no one ever quite usurped the place of Cicely. Dr. Gordon Hake, an old friend of the Marstons, and as a poet the possessor of Philip's admiring regard, has, in his beautiful poem "The Blind Boy," perpetuated the significance of the love of this brother and sister—two exquisite stanzas from which I am tempted to quote—

> "She tells him how the mountains swell,
> How rocks and forests touch the skies;
> He tells her how the shadows dwell
> In purple dimness on his eyes,
> Whose tremulous orbs the while he lifts,
> As round his smile their spirit drifts.
>
> More close around his heart to wind,
> She shuts her eyes in childish glee,
> 'To share,' she said, 'his peace of mind;
> To sit beneath his shadow-tree.'
> So, half in play, the sister tries
> To find his soul within her eyes."

The friend of his own age and sex whose companionship he most cherished at this time (1872), was the late Oliver Madox Brown. An acquaintanceship, much appreciated on either side, developed into a friendship which, to the blind poet especially, meant much. The two young men saw each other regularly ; innumerable literary schemes were talked over ; poems, stories, studies from life were discussed and criticised in Marston's rooms. There one evening Oliver Brown withdrew a bulky MS. from his pocket, informed his friend that an acquaintance had sent him an unpublished romance for his perusal and suggestions, and forthwith began to read the strange and thrilling story of one Gabriel Denver. Once or twice Philip's suspicions were aroused, chiefly on account of the emotion which the reader could not refrain from exhibiting, but still he was unprepared for what followed. The tale excited at once his astonishment and his admiration, and on its conclusion he expressed what he felt in the most emphatic manner.

"What did you say was the name of that story?" he asked.

"*The Black Swan*," was the reply, in a voice husky with emotion.

"And its author? Tell me at once the author's name."

"Oliver Madox Brown."

Sincere were the congratulations, and genuine the mutual joy and pride : that night Oliver went home with a foretaste of fame making his heart beat wildly, while Philip sat awhile in his darkness, and indulged in many a fair visionary dream for his loved friend's future.

When the two were apart, each wrote to the other: in a word, their comradeship was complete, and to the older of the twain it meant more than anything else, save the devotion of his sister Cicely. A deep and all-embracing humour was one of the chief characteristics of Oliver Brown, and he was a delightful *raconteur:* he was thus just the right companion for his blind friend. The latter had of course other friends, among whom may be mentioned his brother-in-law, the late Arthur O'Shaughnessy: indeed, Philip Marston was one of those men possessed of an occult, magnetic quality of attraction which few people could resist. Wherever he went he made would-be friends, and without any apparent effort to please he seemed to exercise a pleasant fascination over all who came in contact with him. And down to the last year of his life he was, in company, cheerful and animated, often merry, and always genial. He never wore his heart upon his sleeve, and even to fairly intimate friends he so rarely betrayed his secret desolation that many of them have been quite unable to realise within what depths of wretchedness his forlorn spirit was wont to dwell. Perhaps there is only one living friend of the dead poet who ever fully knew how dire was the grief and despair which gnawed at his life.

Suddenly Oliver Brown became unwell. Philip was anxious, but never looked for any permanent ill-result. When, all unexpectedly, he was told that Oliver Madox Brown was dead, the shock was so great that years elapsed before he could speak calmly of his loss. Of another bereavement, soon to follow, he never spoke at all. Apart from his keen personal sorrow he deplored the untimely passing away of a young writer of such extraordinarily brilliant promise, believing as he did that no one of such precocious mental powers had appeared since Chatterton.

The young painter-romancist died in 1874. Earlier in the same year was published the second edition of *Song-Tide.* It has been stated in one or two quarters that the pathetic dedication has reference to Miss Nesbit ; this is a mistake, for it is identical with that in the first edition, which appeared before the death of his betrothed. In both editions the dedication has reference to the poet's mother. Nor, it may be added here, are all of the love-sonnets due to Miss Nesbit's inspiration, though doubtless the majority are.

The poems comprised in the volume *All in All* had been read *seriatim* to Oliver Brown, but the book was not actually published till after the latter's death. At best it was a volume of sad memories, and now one of the expected pleasures attendant upon its publication was not to be realised. *All in All* had only a limited success: its sadness was too extreme for the majority of readers, and though, in point of workmanship, it was superior to its predecessor, it was practically voted too gloomy. Some critics went the length of complaining that such a sombre tone as prevailed throughout this volume was either morbid or affected: it is almost needless to say that neither surmise was correct. Irremediable grief, as distinct from more or less placid sorrow, is so rarely experienced by men that it is not strange there should be a tendency to consider it a symptom of weakness or affectation; but few in the place of Philip Marston—unhappy, often lonely, smitten cruelly by adverse fate, and dwelling continually in blank and terrible darkness—would, in all probability, find themselves strongly impelled towards the composition of very joyous verse. We are at best waifs and strays before the wind of circumstance, but when one is whirled hither and thither in absolute darkness the outlook does not become enlivening.

Marston's second volume was dedicated to his father "with profoundest love and admiration." The greater portion of it was occupied by poems in sonnet-form, a fact which possibly conduced towards the book's limited popularity. That the author's attitude was not one of weak despair is manifest from his prefatory words: "In the present volume," he says, "I show how the love, so longed for and despaired of, is at last vouchsafed with all attendant peace and blessedness, until the beloved one is withdrawn, and the mourner is left but a memory, under the inspiration of which he still aspires to some great and far-off good; but is met at every turn by tempters who would mislead, and enemies who would drive back." The author's intention was that *All in All* should form a connecting link between *Song-Tide* and a final section of the series of love-poems to be entitled "A Pilgrimage." The scheme in its entirety was never carried out, though, it may be added, many of the sonnets in *Wind-Voices* were originally intended for the last-named work.

Throughout this second volume it is easy to note how frequently the poet recurs to the theme of irretrievable loss: the lapse of years had blunted the extremity of his pain, but, keen and vital, the old agony was only more subdued, not vanquished. Again, there is to be noted a loyal hope that in the days to come, if he be remembered at all, it may be in union with her whom he had so early lost and so deeply loved:

"When I, at last, with life and love break trust;
When the soul's yearning and the body's lust
Are ended wholly as a tune out-played;
If then, men name my name, and from these lays
The depth and glory of thy soul divine,
Shall not, beloved, my memory live in thine?
Our memories moveless 'mid the moving days,
Intense and sad like changeless stars that shine
On ruined towers of a predestined race."

In this volume also there occurs one of the noblest and most simply direct of Marston's sonnets; one which to all who love and have loved must be of strong and permanent appeal.

NOT THOU BUT I.

It must have been for one of us, my own,
To drink this cup and eat this bitter bread.
Had not my tears upon thy face been shed,
Thy tears had dropped on mine; if I alone
Did not walk now, thy spirit would have known
My loneliness, and did my feet not tread
This weary path and steep, thy feet had bled
For mine, and thy mouth had for mine made moan;
And so it comforts me, yea, not in vain,
To think of thy eternity of sleep,
To know thine eyes are tearless though mine weep:
And when this cup's last bitterness I drain,
One thought shall still its primal sweetness keep—
Thou hadst the peace and I the undying pain.

The saddest life is not without compensations: at least, this somewhat hackneyed saying may pass as a generalisation. Few men have ever had more friends than the blind poet of whom I write; men and women of the most opposite tastes and sympathies were at one in their regard and love for Philip Marston.

"There *is* a kind of compensation," he remarked to me once, "in the way that new friendships arise to brighten my life as soon as I am bowled over by some great loss. But one's capacities for friendship get worn out, and it is impossible that I can ever be to new friends that which I was to those who are gone and am still to the one or two who are left."

About this time Marston came to know Dante Gabriel Rossetti with something like intimacy. No man ever obtained from him more fervent, it may without exaggeration be said more worshipful regard. As a poet he considered Rossetti foremost among those of the Victorian age, and his love for him as a man was deep and abiding. Nothing prejudiced a stranger quicker in his view than disparagement of Rossetti: admiration of the author of *The House of Life*, on the other hand, was a bond of immediate union. For Mr. Swinburne, also, he always entertained emphatic admiration and strong personal regard, and among his few most-valued friendships was that with Mr. Theodore Watts. None of these, however, he saw with any frequency; hence, after the death of Oliver Madox Brown, he found himself in growing solitude.

It was subsequently to the publication of *All in All* that Marston began to write for the American magazines, his first acceptance coming from the editor of *Scribner's Magazine.* From this time forth he more and more devoted himself to production for the American public, with the result that he is now far more widely known as a poet and writer of fiction in the United States than in Great Britain. He would fain have had it otherwise, but his poems and stories met with almost invariable rejection in this country, and he became wearied of what appeared to be a hopeless attempt. Moreover, he had to live, for his means had become straitened. Anyhow, it came to pass that nine-tenths of his prose-writings and the great proportion of his short poems appeared in American journals and magazines; and that this writer of exquisite verse experienced nothing but disappointment on the hither side of the Atlantic.

In 1876, as has already been recorded, he made the acquaintance of Mrs. Louise Chandler Moulton. The friendship arose from and was sustained upon a keen literary and intellectual sympathy. Mrs. Moulton was interested from the outset in the young poet and his work, and Marston was soon attracted to one who evinced such kindly interest and consideration. The affectionate devotion of this most loyal and helpful of his friends did more than anything else to cheer his remaining years. In Mrs. Moulton, he not only found the most perfect intellectual sympathy; her broad and cultured taste, her wide experience of the world of men and women and of the world of books, and the charm of her society, all helped —as he said himself—to make life endurable. Every spring Mrs. Moulton came to London for the season: during her visits the blind poet forgot much of his weary sadness, and even the long months of absence were relieved by continuous correspondence. It would have fared ill with him in his latter years if it had not been for the self-sacrificing and sisterly care of this devoted friend.

This friendship was formed in time, for it was not long afterward that Marston endured another great loss—one of the most deeply felt afflictions of his life. Mrs. Moulton, as will be seen, has best right to speak of this event, so I shall let the narration be in her words. "I had known him and his sister but a few days more than two years when, on July 28, 1878, Cicely called upon me at my rooms. Dr. Marston and Philip were away in

France, and she spoke of them very tenderly that morning. She complained, when she came in, of an intense headache, and after a little I made her lie down to see what rest would do for her. She grew worse, and when the doctor came he pronounced her illness apoplexy. My name was the last word on her faithful lips ; and in the mid-afternoon of that long July day she died. Quite unaware of her death—since we did not know where to find them with a telegram—and while she was still awaiting burial, her father and brother returned. On this crushing sorrow I cannot linger. Its full bitterness I shared. I think it was the cruellest bereavement that had ever come to our poet. When his mother, his betrothed, and his friend died, he still—as he used often to say—had Cicely ; but when she left him there remained for him no such constant and consoling presence. His other sister was married, and therefore was not in his daily life at all ; and at that time, even she herself was a chronic invalid. His father was his one closest tie ; but many sorrows had saddened Dr. Marston and broken his health ; and there was no one to be to Philip what Cicely had been, as reader, amanuensis, and constant untiring companion. It was the year before Cicely's death (1877) in which, to gratify a whim of mine, the well-know novelist, R. E. Francillon, cast Philip's horoscope. Mr. Francillon is a loving student of all mystic lore, and has studied astrology by way of amusing himself, until he has become a thorough proficient in its mysteries. As a sort of test of the clear seeing of the stars, I persuaded him to cast, and carefully to write out, the horoscope of the blind poet ; and in this manuscript—which I still have in my possession—he prophesied, several times over, the death of its subject in 1887. One never believes in such prophecies until after their fulfilment ; but I look back, now, to see, with wonder, how many predictions, even besides this final one, that horoscope contained ; and they have been fulfilled, every one."

In that dreary year after the death of his beloved sister, life seemed to him a bitter and worthless thing. Mrs. Moulton had returned to America, Oliver Brown was dead, his father—a beloved companion and friend—was in ill-health.* Desolate in spirit and sorely tried in mind and body, Marston sought surcease of pain in hard work. Literature was his saving : without it he had perished.

* There is one statement in Mrs. Moulton's narration that is misleading. From Cicely's death to that of her brother Dr. Marston *did* affectionately and faithfully act as his son's reader, amanuensis, and constant untiring companion.

Although those sea-coast and inland voyages wherein he was wont to take such keen delight were still indulged in, they no longer pleased as of yore. In his own pathetic words, as he spoke to me on the subject some years ago, he had undergone the experience of twice becoming blind. His own sight waned in childhood and was drowned in tears in his early manhood; his second sight, his sister Cicely, was snatched from him with more terrible suddenness.

It was about the beginning of 1880 that I came to know Philip Marston. In the autumn of the preceding year I was spending an evening with Rossetti, and I chanced to make some reference to Marston's poetry. Finding that I did not know the blind poet and that I was anxious to meet him, Rossetti promised to bring us together; one thing and another, however, intervened to prevent our speedy meeting. At last, one day in January, I reminded Rossetti of his promise, and the result was a line of introduction posted direct to Marston. I remember that I was fascinated by him at once—his manner, his personality, his conversation. On his part he gave a generous reception to one who had no claim to his regard save acquaintanceship with the poet for whom we had in common the most genuine love and reverence. Our friendship grew steadily—but I need not say more of it here than that with his death I have lost a very dear and valued friend.

A year had not passed since the decease of Cicely, when fresh sorrows came in the guise of the deaths of his sister Nellie (Mrs. O'Shaughnessy) and her two children. Marston now saw more of Arthur O'Shaughnessy. One day in 1881 I was sitting with the former, when O'Shaughnessy ran into the room, reminded me of a promise to go to his house and hear him read the proof-sheets of his new book, and asked his brother-in-law to come also. In less than a week, poor O'Shaughnessy was dead: sudden and fatal inflammation of the lungs had put an end to all his hopes and dreams.

At Eastertide in the ensuing year Rossetti's death came upon Marston with a great shock. I had been staying at Birchington shortly before the end came, and not foreseeing the imminent disaster, had brought back not unhopeful news; and, at Rossetti's request, I also planned to go down to Kent again with Philip. We did indeed journey thither shortly, but it was to attend the funeral of him whom we both so loved and admired. Now more than ever he began to believe that a malign fate had foredoomed all his most cherished friendships to disastrous endings. Looking through the letters which during periods of absence he addressed to me, I find this note of apprehension ever recurring. He had a vague, half-real belief, which was not altogether fanciful, that he had lived the human life on earth before. This idea is embodied in the following sonnet which he addressed to me in the first year of our friendship, the publication of which in this place may on this illustrative account be excused.

MET BEFORE.

Not surely now for the first time we meet:
  So seems it to me, rather I believe
  That in some vanished state one had to grieve
For loss of other, and with weary feet
Went on his way finding no sweet thing sweet,
  Listless and sad, unwilling to reprieve
  His thoughts from pain by joys that but deceive,
Nor trusting to a friendship less complete:
At length through death into new life he passed;
  And there he joined his friend, then hand clasp'd hand,
Then soul cried out to soul, re-met at last;
  So seemeth it to us, who understand
Each other perfectly, and know right well
How much there is on either side to tell.

It was in 1882, also, that another friend, to whom Marston had become much attached—attracted in the first instance by the common bond of unhappiness—died under peculiarly distressing circumstances. The public who are interested in that strange and sombre poem, "The City of

Dreadful Night," know vaguely that James Thomson died in poverty and in some obscure fashion. Philip Marston and myself were, if I am not mistaken, the last of his acquaintances who saw him alive. Thomson had suffered such misery and endured such hopelessness, that he had yielded to intemperate habits, including a frequent excess in the use of opium. He had come back from a prolonged visit to the country, where all had been well with him, but through over-confidence he had fallen a victim again immediately on his return. For a few weeks his record is almost a blank. When the direst straits were reached, he so far reconquered his control that he felt himself able to visit one whose sympathy and regard had withstood all tests. The latter soon realised that his friend was mentally distraught, and endured a harrowing experience, into the narration of which I do not care to enter. I arrived in the late afternoon, and found Marston in a state of nervous perturbation. Thomson was lying down on the bed in the adjoining room : stooping, I caught his whispered words to the effect that he was dying ; upon which I lit a match, and in the sudden glare beheld his white face on the blood-stained pillow. He had burst one or more blood-vessels, and the hæmorrhage was dreadful. Some time had to elapse before anything could be done, but ultimately, with the help of a friend who came in opportunely, poor Thomson was carried downstairs and, having been placed in a cab, was driven to the adjoining University Hospital. He did not die that night, nor when Marston and I went to see him in the ward the next day was he perceptibly worse, but a few hours after our visit he passed away. Thus came to an end the saddest life with which I have ever come in contact—sadder even than that of Philip Marston, though *his* existence was oftentimes bitter enough to endure.

I do not regret this opportunity for narrating simply and directly the circumstances attendant upon James Thomson's illness and death. I have several times heard, and once or twice seen in print, such misleading statements that in justice to his friends as well as to the dead it was but fitting I should briefly give the main outlines of a painful incident.

Thomson's death, and the manner of it, affected Marston very deeply. To a man of his sensitive nature, the very room where his friend had lain when his death-stroke came upon him was haunted by something inexplicable, but tragic and oppressive. This sense of haunted rooms—in a somewhat vaguer, yet not less genuine significance than the epithet generally bears—was a very real thing to him. It was for this reason that one of his favourites among Rossetti's sonnets was that entitled "Memorial Thresholds." Readers of the poems will find numerous passages which give expression to it: indeed, some of his most pathetic verses were evolved from this motive.

"Must this not be, that one then dwelling here,
Where one man and his sorrows dwelt so long,
Shall feel the pressure of a ghostly throng,
And shall upon some desolate midnight hear
A sound more sad than is the pine-trees' song,
And thrill with great, inexplicable fear?"

Probably no one has ever felt more grateful to the inventor of the "type-writer" than did Philip Marston. When he purchased, and learned the method of working, one of those invaluable machines, he found himself to a great extent independent of an amanuensis. By this means he wrote all his stories and poems, and also his extensive correspondence, without assistance from any one. It was, naturally, a matter of no little moment to him to be able to write, enfold, and address private letters without having to place expressions meant for one person within view of another. For a considerable period he spelt for the most part phonetically, but in course of time he came to write as correctly as most educated people.

Dr. Westland Marston revised the type-written sheets meant for publication.

The blind poet was a rapid as well as an industrious worker. From his slight and late breakfast (for from his boyhood he had been accustomed to go to bed at times when the mass of his fellow-citizens had been asleep for some hours) the *click-click* of his type-writing machine might be heard incessantly till far on in the afternoon. By dinner-time a goodly array of foolscap pages would environ his chair, and several letters would lie on the adjoining table awaiting postage.

He also became proficient in the Braïlle system, but was unable to gain much satisfaction therefrom, owing to the fact that few of his friends at a distance could bring themselves to learn it sufficiently for correspondence. He never, however, urged his wish upon his absent acquaintances, for he was quite aware of the much greater difficulty in the acquirement of the Braïlle and allied systems experienced by those who had use of their eyes, and whose finger-nerves were, comparatively, so much more insensitive.

As each year elapsed Marston found his reputation in America more and more assured. His stories and poems not only gained acceptance at the hands of editors, but procured for him many friends. After Mrs. Moulton, and another kind and generous friend, Mrs. L. C. Bullard, the friend of oversea whom he most valued was the "Poet of the South," Paul Hamilton Hayne; for Whittier, E. C. Stedman, R. W. Gilder, and others, he had a sincere regard. A glance at the books in his room at No. 191 Euston Road would have convinced any new-comer as to his numerous friends and admirers. From many well-known, slightly-known, and quite unknown poets and novelists of both sexes, there were scores of volumes containing on their fly-leaves affectionate and flattering inscriptions. Nothing of this kind was more valued by him than Swinburne's and Rossetti's books, given to him by their authors. There was something very pathetic in the ardent and unbroken friendship between Paul Hamilton Hayne and his English comrade. Their correspondence was continuous, and most of their letters were lengthy epistles. Both eagerly anticipated meeting. Perhaps at last their long friendship has its consummation, for Hayne died in the autumn of 1886. His death was yet another keenly-felt sorrow for the friend who survived him for a few weary months.*

* A short time after his son's death Dr. Westland Marston received a gracious tribute from that Southern State where Paul Hamilton Hayne spent most of his life. Many of the admirers of Philip Marston's poetry—with recognition

During the spring months of 1884 I was residing at Dover, and in April (if I remember aright) Marston came down from London to spend a week or so with me. The weather was perfect, and our walks by shore and cliff were full of delight to us both: once or twice we crossed to Calais for the sake of the sail, spent a few hours in the old French port, and returned by the afternoon boat. In the evenings, after dinner, we invariably adjourned to the beach, either under the eastern bluffs or along the base of Shakespeare's Cliff, for the music of the sea, in calm or tidal turbulence or tempest, had an unfailing fascination for him.

He took keen pleasure in learning how to distinguish the songs of the different birds, and all spring's sounds and scents were sources of exquisite pleasure. How well I remember the rapt expression of puzzled delight which animated his face, as one day we crossed some downs to the westward of Folkestone.

"Oh, what is that?" he cried, eagerly; and, to my surprise, I found that what had so excited him was the crying of the young lambs as they stumbled

also of the friendship between the American poet and his English comrade—sent a large lyre made of white immortelles, with the word *Marston* in purple flowers across the strings. I may add here that in *Wind-Voices* there is a pathetic sonnet addressed to Hayne.

or frisked about their mothers. He had so seldom been out of London in the early spring that so common an incident as this had all the charm of newness to him. A frisky youngster was easily enticed alongside, and the blind poet's almost child-like happiness in playing with the woolly little creature was something delightful to witness. A little later I espied one which had only been a few hours in the world, and speedily placed it in his arms. He would fain have carried it away with him ; in his tender solicitude for it he was like a mother over her first-born.

As we turned to walk homeward we met a boy holding a young starling in his hand. Its feeble, strident cries, its funny little beak closing upon his finger under the impression it was a gigantic worm, delighted him almost as much as the lambkin. "A day of days!" was his expressive commentary, as tired and hungry we reached home and sat down to dinner, with the deep boom of the sea clearly audible through the open window.

Marston had a subtle sympathy with nature which amounted almost to a new sense. A cloud would rise upon the horizon, and he would be the first to portend some change in the weather; it was as if his sightless eyes yet conveyed some message to his mind, or as if his ears heard an ominous murmur of far-off wind and rain inaudible to senses less acute. Sunset, a solemn moon-rise, the company of cloud-drifts passing westward and glowing with delicate and gorgeous tones and hues, to these he was never insensitive, even if no friend referred to them ; in some occult fashion he seemed to be aware that these things were making earth and heaven beautiful.

There is none among our younger poets who has touched with more exquisite truth and grace those evanescent aspects of the skies, those soft fleeting hues of earth and sea ; the inner vision of the blind poet was as faithful to him as the pole-star to the seaman.

And because to him the sea and the wind were always among the most wonderful things in nature, endlessly suggestive, endlesslv beautiful to eye and ear and spirit, his love for them never grew less. But in the growing sadness of his latter years one of his most abiding sorrows was the loss, in great part, of the old passionate love and yearning for nature. But for his blindness this would not have been so, for to men and women who have anything in them of spiritual life, nature is the source of their most sacred comfort. On a mountain-slope, on a wide plain, by the margin of the sea, the keenest grief becomes rarefied till it attains to a higher and nobler plane of sorrow.

Far more deeply than some of his friends

guessed did he feel this passing away of the old worship. It was a genuine sorrow to him, a deep and cruel disappointment. "It is as though one were parting with one's last hope—one's sole remaining consolation," he once remarked to me bitterly. In the sonnet called "Youth and Nature" (*p.* 177) he has given expression to this sense of estrangement.

Few natural incidents seemed to strike him more ominously and painfully than the oncoming in mid-July of one of those autumnal winds which make one vaguely realise that the summer is dying. The sonnet, "A July Day" (*p.* 178), was born of this emotional susceptibility.

Even Spring, for which he ever yearned throughout the rest of the year, brought with it latterly but little of that conscious and unconscious exhilaration which it is wont to bring to all of us. "Spring Sadness" was his theme rather than "Spring Joy." In the fine and pathetic sonnet entitled "In Early Spring" (*p.* 176) this sad foreknowledge of its significance is recorded.

The three sonnets just referred to are from the third of Philip Marston's published volumes of poetry. In 1883-84 this book was issued by Mr. Elliot Stock, with the poetic title *Wind-Voices.* Its success was immediate and emphatic. Messrs.

Roberts Bros., of Boston, speedily disposed of every copy of the American edition, and the London publisher sold the last few score at a considerable premium. The book is consequently almost as difficult to obtain as *Song-Tide*, for it was not stereotyped.

Wind-Voices is dedicated to "Louise Chandler Moulton, True Poet and True Friend." It contains much that is very beautiful and very touching, and exhibits a greater breadth and *grip* than its predecessors. I am hardly likely to be contradicted in the assertion that it contains a greater amount of genuine poetry than any volume by the best known of Marston's contemporaries of about his own age.

In addition to a further instalment of his exquisite flower-lyrics, grouped under the title "Garden Secrets" *(see page 199)*, there are touching poems in memory of Oliver Madox Brown, Arthur O'Shaughnessy, James Thomson, and Rossetti, and several sonnets addressed to C. N. M. (his sister Cicely). Among the more ambitious poems are "Caedmon," where the Saxon poet relates before the Abbess Hilda that famous dream which resulted in the Song of Creation; "Caught in the Nets" *(see page 264)*, a merman story founded on a passage in Sir Richard Baker's "Chronicle," wherein is described the capture of a strange, half-human creature of the deep, on the Suffolk coast in the twelfth century, and its ultimate escape to the "dear waves" and "some sea-girl's damp and salt caresses;" "The Ballad of the Monk Julius" *(p. 271)*, based on the familiar legend of the demon-tempted monk; the "Ballad of Brave Women" *(p. 248)*, a record of two heroic Swansea fishermen's wives, which, however, is too markedly Rossettian; and "Nightshade," founded on the conclusion of Oliver Madox Brown's "Dwale Bluth," as designed though not completed by its author. The songs and lyrics scattered throughout the volume are most winsome. Those beginning "Now that Hope lies sick to death," and "Love has turned his face away" *(see "Three Songs," p. 303)*, have much of the subtle charm of the lyrics of the Elizabethan poets. "The Old Churchyard of Bonchurch" *(p. 259)*, headed by a note stating that "this old churchyard has been for many years slipping toward the sea, which it is expected will ultimately engulf it," has an exquisite music in it recalling the happiest effects of Poe and Swinburne.

The sonnets, of which there is a large number, are unequal: yet some of the poet's finest are in *Wind-Voices*, and perhaps nowhere has he written one more powerfully imaginative than that entitled "No Death" *(p. 195)*.

His health henceforth steadily declined. His power of concentration lessened, and all labour became a weariness to him. "It is impossible I can live long," he was wont to exclaim, impatiently—"how unutterably thankful I would be for the end, if only—if only—I *knew* what lay beyond!"

Until the summer of 1886, however, he still wrote industriously, though rarely in verse. In August he and his father were at Brighton for rest and change of air. Every autumn for some years past, it may be mentioned here, father and son went away somewhere together; neither was wont to tire of the other's companionship, for the friendship between them was almost as brotherly and amicable as paternal and filial. One hot day, while bareheaded in the glare of the sun, Philip was prostrated by a heat-stroke, which was followed by serious illness of an epileptiform nature. Mind and body suffered from the strain, and the derangement foretold death.

So great was his vitality and power of endurance that neither his father nor the friends who saw him at this time guessed the imminence of the end. Mrs. Moulton was disturbed by his condition, but when she sailed for America early in October she foresaw no final breakdown.

Throughout the winter his letters were full of foreboding and weariness. "You will miss me, perhaps, when I am gone, but you must not mourn for me. I think few lives have been so deeply sad as mine, though I do not forget those who have blessed it." This was the keynote of each infinitely sad letter. About mid-winter he wrote to Mrs. Moulton, "I feel that I said my last good-bye to you, that 4th of October, when we parted at the Euston Station. I shall be gone—somewhere—before you come again. The stony streets will be here, and the bells that drive me mad will ring; but *I* shall be gone. You will miss me sometimes, I think, you and a few others; and perhaps people will be sorry when they remember how dark and lonely was the life I lived here." Again, "If I *could* only sleep. I try everything, but rest will not come. Is there anything in all the world so good as sleep."

Serious illness and months of tardy convalescence prevented my seeing anything of Marston from the spring of 1886 until December. On Christmas forenoon I went to see and spend an hour or so with him. He was in bed, and I was shocked by the change. It was almost imperceptible to those who had lately seen much of him, but as nearly a year had elapsed since I had seen him (save for a few minutes on one or two occasions), I found the alteration only too evident.

On the last day of January 1887 paralysis set

in, and gradually the nervous system surrendered. For the next fourteen days the invalid lay speechless, as well as sightless. His efforts to make himself understood were at times most harrowing. Certain wishes he managed to convey, but latterly his will-power was insufficient even for the tremulous raising of his wasted hand in sign of acquiescence or negation. To another friend and myself I know that he consciously bade farewell: blind though he was he saw the shadow of death coming very near.

On Sunday, February 13th, the restlessness had gone, and he spent a better night than he had done for long. It was that strange apathy which sometimes precedes the final energy of the act of death. On Monday morning, about 9.45, he suffered from a momentary palpitation; gave one or two low sighs, and was gone.

All the fever and fret of his life had passed out of his face on the day when he was laid in his coffin. At last he was asleep and at peace.

On Friday, the day of the funeral, the few friends who were asked to attend felt, on taking a farewell glance at the face of the dead poet, that Death had never looked more beautiful. Pure and white, with the pallor but not with the rigidity of marble, the serene face lay amidst white flowers which intertwined with the dark hair and beard. Among the many wreaths which had been sent from far and near were one or two where the laurel prevailed, so that in death also he went honoured as was his due.

Philip Bourke Marston was buried at Highgate cemetery. Having belonged to no sect in matters of religion, and having expressed a desire to have no regular ritual at his grave—though in him, I may say here, abode that large faith in ultimate good which is the vital spirit of all true religions—he was lowered to his rest after a few earnest words from an old and valued friend of himself and his father.

It seems fitting to say somewhat here concerning the personality of Philip Marston.

Close upon five feet eleven in height, his erect carriage and alert attitude afforded him a buoyant and youthful aspect. His features were clearly-cut, his sensitive mouth very mobile, and the expression—until the last year or so, when illness wrought such ravage upon him—one of peculiar refinement and very winning. He was always slight, and latterly was fragile, in figure ; his hands were a musician's, supple, long-fingered, delicate. This last remark reminds me how passionately fond he was of music : I have seen him quivering like an aspen-leaf under its influence. He played a little by ear upon the pianoforte, mainly old plaintive airs, illusive reminiscences of those folk-strains which have usually so much of the *vox humana* in their melodies.

Marston was generosity itself; hospitality he was wont to exercise to excess. His faculty of putting himself *en rapport* with the prevailing mood of his company was electric, and it is this, doubtless, which has led so many of his acquaintances to think, on the one hand, that his most intimate friends have exaggerated his habitual spiritual gloom; and, on the other, that his unhappiness has not by them been sufficiently emphasised.

It may be said, in a word, that his customary bearing towards his friends was one of animation and interest; that his habitual attitude, for himself, was one of almost invariable gloom and deep despondency. His interests dwelt mainly with literature; supremely with poetry.

Work is the surest palliative for a broken heart, and in arduous and incessant labour, as has been already stated, the blind poet found some measure of relief. In his later years his idea of possible happiness was to be independent of literary work; to live in an old manor completely shut off from the outside world by orchards, old-fashioned fragrant-flowered gardens, and shady avenues of elm and beech; to be within a short walk of the sea ; there to write nothing but poetry, and then only when the impulse was irresistible ; and there to have occasional friendly visits from dwellers in distant Babylon. He dwelt on this halcyon existence with a half-humorous, half-yearning persistency which showed how keen was his longing for some such peaceful passing of his remaining years. "Just imagine," he would say, "what it would mean to be beyond reach of this everlasting Babel of the Euston Road! Instead of cabs and omnibusses and the jangling din of those accursed bells, to hear such blessed and soothing sounds as the rustling of leaves and the swaying of boughs ; the cawing of rooks and the drowsy cooing of the wood-doves ; the wind passing over the grass, and the ever-varying music of the sea!" No such sweet nepenthê was to be his, however, poor fellow.

The ear accustoms itself wonderfully to any noisiness that is incessant, and of the endless tumult of the busy Euston Road Marston became practically heedless ; but to the intermittent yet far from infrequent clangour of the church, chapel, and other bells he never grew resigned. In one of his latest sonnets, if not as I believe *the* latest, he refers to these hated bells. This sonnet is published in *Lippincott's Magazine* for April 1887. Appearing just six weeks after the poet's death,

"My Grave" seems a sadly appropriate last utterance, a pathetic "music at the close."

MY GRAVE.

For me no great metropolis of the dead,—
Highways and byways, squares and crescents of death,—
But, after I have breathed my last sad breath,
Am comforted with quiet, I who said,
"I weary of men's voices and their tread,
Of clamouring bells, and whirl of wheels that pass,"
Lay me beneath some plot of country grass,
Where flowers may spring, and birds sing overhead:
Whereto one coming, some fair eve in spring,
Between the day-fall and the tender night,
Might pause awhile, his friend remembering,
And hear low words breathed through the failing light,
Spoken to him by the wind, whispering,
"Now he sleeps long, who had so long to fight."

I wrote, a few sentences back, of Marston's ideal of possible happiness during his later years. In his boyhood, youth, and early manhood all his desires were towards action. He had then no craving for rest, for the iron had not yet entered into his soul sufficiently to paralyse each faculty save that of endurance. The soldier, the mariner, the pioneer—those were the men whom he envied most. *To be doing*—that was his keenest desire. In all stories of adventure, real and fictitious, he took great delight. For a long period during his youth he lived a kind of dual existence. His father has told me how Philip was "always off somewhere"—India, China, America, Australia, the North and South Polar Seas, the Pacific, and so forth. In those imaginary voyages he was invariably accompanied by two jovial and dare-devil personages whom he had named Buffalo and Mackintosh. In the daring exploits upon the high seas, in the wild scenes in unexplored countries, in the terrific combats with bloodthirsty savages, Buffalo and Mackintosh were often temporarily prostrated; but they were always to hand for any new voyage when their creator required them. Both "worthies" continued to be faithful companions for many years, and when at last they died a natural death, their memories remained evergreen. Philip always enjoyed a reference to the daring Buffalo and the redoubtable Mackintosh, and, I suspect, oftentimes joined them again in the land of shades and revelled in many a surreptitious adventure. Although his poetic development was precocious, he had no wish "to sit at home and write poetry." When the glamour of recent association with Buffalo and Mackintosh was not upon him, he would yearn even for the unromantic life of a city clerk. Anything to be doing: that was his one cry until it changed into "anything for rest."

Nothing is more surprising than the maturity of thought and expression which occasionally characterises the productions of young poets who have in them something of the divine breath of genius. As already mentioned, such fine poems as "A Christmas Vigil" and "The Rose and the Wind" —indeed most of the poems in *Song-Tide*— were written before the poet's twentieth birthday: several of his published sonnets were composed between the ages of fourteen and eighteen. That entitled "Desolate" (*vide p.* 91) was written during the author's fifteenth year.

"A Christmas Vigil," written in Marston's nineteenth year, is beyond question a remarkable poem for so young a man: its dramatic vision and intensity, its poetic concision, its humanity, combine in irresistible appeal. In this sad story of a ruined woman's life there are passages displaying that exquisite insight into and sympathy with external nature which Philip Marston, blind though he was, so frequently demonstrated. This is hardly a stanza such as we would expect from a blind man:

"Now, when the time of the sun's setting came,
The sky caught flame;
For all the sun, which as an empty name
Had been that day, then rent the leaden veil
And flashed out sharp, 'twixt watery clouds, and pale;

Then, suddenly, a stormy wind upsprang,
That shrieked and sang ;
Around the reeling tree-tops loud it rang,
And all was dappled blue, and faint, fresh gold,
Lovely, and virgin ; wild, and sweet, and cold."

But neither in *Wind-Voices* nor in either of its successors is there anything more memorable than the exquisite lyric, "The Rose and the Wind," (*vide p.* 200). It is in point of substance as well as in manner very remarkable as the work of a youth. In a letter which Rossetti wrote to its author occurs the following passage of genuine as well as generous praise : "Only yesterday evening I was reading your 'Garden Secrets' to William Bell Scott, who fully agreed with me that it was not too much to say of them that they are worthy of Shakespeare in his subtlest lyrical moods."

The stories included in the volume entitled *For a Song's Sake** represent about a third—possibly rather more—of Marston's short tales. These stories their author was wont to speak of, half in fun, as his Prose Bitters. Though a posthumous publication, it was in accordance with the author's own wish that the volume bore the name of the first and longest tale in the collection. The book was dedicated to "the many admirers, here and in

* Cloth, Crown 8vo, price 4s. 6d. Walter Scott.

America, of the poet and writer, and to all who hold the man in loving remembrance."

And thus all is over for Philip Bourke Marston —the long toil, the abiding pain, the infinite weariness. Many years ago, while he was in the prime of youth, tears quenched the flickering flame of light in his dimmed eyes: through a darker gloom than any in which he travailed here he has passed towards the light.

Looking at his serene face on the day ere the coffin-lid enclosed it, where something lovelier than mortal sleep subtly dwelt, there was one at least of his friends who forgot all sorrow in a great gladness for the blind poet—now no longer blind, if he be not overwhelmed in a sleep beyond our ken. At such a moment the infinite satisfaction of Death seems bountiful largess for the turmoil of a few "dark, disastrous years."

Wheresoever he who is gone from us now is, surely it is well with him.

> "Far off is he, above desire or fear:
> No more subjected to the change or chance
> Of the unsteady planets."

Among the minor poets of the day—and of course I use the word "minor" not in any derogatory but simply in the proper sense of the term—there is none who excels Marston as a sonneteer or lyricist. The very great advance displayed in his latest volume would seem to point to what an assuredly permanent place he would have taken among Victorian poets had the mischances and brevity of his life not proved adverse to the high hopes entertained of him by those best fitted to judge the scope and limitations of his genius. As a writer of narrative poetry, I do not think that he would have ever distinguished himself. The sonnet and the lyric were the metrical forms which most appealed to him, not only as a writer but as a reader of verse: and this, doubtless, from the circumstance that his own poetic impulse was of the intensely subjective order. Nor does it seem to me that he would ever have ranked really high among the poets of his time in the composition of dramatic ballads, as it was his ambition to do. Poems like "A Christmas Vigil" or the "Ballad of Brave Women," lyrics showing such keen and searching insight as "The Rose and the Wind," at first sight display a promise for which it would scarcely be rash to predicate genuine poetic greatness: yet it may well be doubted if they really do so. Marston's poetic insight is subtle in only one direction : it is love—sexual love, in the broadest sense—that is the magnet of his poetic energy. He nowhere in his poems, or in his prose tales, manifests any depth of vision into the life of nature or of man, save in the direction indicated. He did not or could not acquire genuine knowledge of the great motors and complex issues of human nature in general : circumstances, to a great extent, militated against his poetic development through direct personal experience, and he was ever—it seemed to me at least—averse from, or at any rate, indifferent to that vicarious experience which, when acquired with the subtle discrimination of genius, is often as valuable as, occasionally more valuable than, what is learnt through personal participation. Marston's poetry is in the main monotonous, not merely because it deals chiefly with sexual love, and more particularly with the sad or sombre aspects of passionate affection, but also, and perhaps primarily, because of the lack of what his friend and master Rossetti called fundamental brain-work. A great poet might write a hundred sonnets upon the aspects of a single sexual passion, and yet never become monotonous : such an one could only charm us continually by abstinence from any mere harping on one string, however dexterous the minor variations in which he might indulge. If he were unable to draw upon an immense reserve of accumulated knowledge of life, if his intellect were not free to soar eagle-like across wide realms of thought and continents of historic experience, as well as to dart blithely and lightly as the swallow through the common air of the familiar world—if, in a word, he were not abreast of the philosophical and scientific knowledge of his time, as well as actually and vicariously aware of all the emotions and sensations of varied life, it would be almost impossible for him, though his subjectivity were as intense as Heine's, and his poetic impulse as irresistible as that of Burns, to dwell without becoming monotonous, through a long sequence of artificial verse, upon the joys and woes of his individual love. "What can a man put into his verse?" touches a much more important matter than "How is he going to express himself?" although, of course, blindness to or even injudicious neglect of the exigencies of form can readily be fatal to the perpetuity of what had else well deserved survival. Doubtless, in the deepest sense, poetry, as has often been said, *is* form; but this is so very radical a definition that it may best be left to those whom alone it concerns—the critical specialists who prate so much of originality, but whose dicta, if in universal application, would be as a ban upon all fresh and independent poetic impulse. No wise student of literature, least of all any genuine poet, despises the just trammels, the needful limitations imposed by the exigent demand of form; and he who would achieve a measure of fame for any self-loved utterance must pay all due heed to the vehicle of his ideas, so that it offend none by ungainliness or by lack of that refined taste whereof 'form' is the prime manifestation. But, after all, substance is the main thing, howsoever it may be called — 'substance,' 'matter,' 'intellectual basis,' 'intensity and scope of mental vision,' 'fundamental brainwork.' If, as Keats declared, invention be the pole-star of poetry, intellectual basis may be likened to the moon that lifts and directs the innumerable waves of song upon the sea of life. Of course it goes without saying that "intellectuality" is not poetry, nor even the first essential of poetry. Poetry is the outcome of an intellectual or sensuous emotion felt with such rhythmic vibration, as it were, that no other result than metrical music be possible. It is, or should be, the flower of life, the quintessence of direct or apprehended experience. It must be spontaneous in its birth, free in its movement, impulsive in its spirit. It may exist as delicately, as transiently, as a butterfly over the hour-long bloom of the cistus, or it may live and endure with the hardihood of a pine-tree fronting the blasts of centuries. Sweet are the fleeting wood-notes-wild of song, but only those which are the outcome of quintessential life can survive the stress of time. For this quintessential life, what is it but the concentring, the focussing of all the rays of human knowledge and experience into an overwhelmingly vivid beam of light: and it is in the perception of this light, and the manifold endeavours to translate something of its radiance, that the idiosyncracies of the true poet find fit development. One will express with the dramatic vigour of Shakespeare, one with the piercing subtlety of Goethe; another with the intense personal note of Catullus, or Heine, or Shelley, yet another with the lyric lilt of Burns or Béranger; one will soar with Milton, or dally as lightly as Herrick in his miry Devon—another will achieve his aim through the worldly wisdom of Browning, or not less surely through "the colossal innocence" of Blake. A poem must not always show its intellectual basis, any more than a body must show its soul ere its mortal beauty be allowed to win our allegiance. But just as the loveliness of a woman is dominated by the expression which animates the features, and not by the mere contours and lines and all the physiognomic charm of youth, so the final, the supreme merit of a poem is not in any perfection of art, but in the union thereof with something higher still—an original, vivid, vital thought.

By natural instinct and capacity, Marston had a true sense of form, though this inherent capacity—developed and intensified as it was by practice and external literary influences—manifested itself irregularly and unequally. Poetry at no time became for him a mere matter of pleasurable or profitable verse-making: it was the one pure and perfect thing in a life of soilure and distress—a sacred divinity among many fallen idols. But occasionally the impulse was too slight to overreach the dividing line betwixt absolute and comparative poetry: at times the inspiration failed, though so skilful had the craftsman become, that only those with keen and immediate insight perceived the distinction between what was artistically inevitable and what was masterfully manufactured.

It is in the sonnet that Marston's genius is supposed to show itself most unmistakably. These sonnets of his, at their best, have qualities which, in the main, would justify a critic in his placement of them extremely high in the sonnet-literature of the later Victorian period—perhaps, even, in ranking them as superior to those of any other contemporary poet, after the sonorous and intensely artistic series by the author of *The House of Life*.

But it is precisely because of their affinity to the latter that no continuity of poetic repute can be foretold of them. Beautiful as most of them are, masterly as are a few, one and all bear witness to the fact that Marston as a sonneteer is but the satellite of a greater poetic luminary than himself. Yet in this there is no implication of mere imitativeness. A poet's genius may be markedly derivative, and may nevertheless have such qualities of insight, music, beauty, and even distinction, that his productions will be wronged if they be not acknowledged and welcomed for their own sake. But when a poet is, as it were, under the shadow of so dominant and impressive a master as Rossetti, it were vain to suppose that he could ever rank higher than, at best, the foremost of the disciples. And it is in itself a proof that Marston had genius when we consider that, poetic thrall as he was to Rossetti as a sonneteer, he was yet able to be in a great measure himself, to give to his work the stamp of his own domination even while wavering not in lealty to his overlord. For in his many sonnets there is much that is exceedingly fine, much even that he might fairly claim for distinctively his own; and had he been less susceptible to an unique ideal, had he striven more arduously towards individual distinction in style, he would in all probability have won a crown of long-lived laurel. Even as it is, there are many of his sonnets which will long endure with us, and there are one or two, *Not Thou But I* for instance, which are assured of perpetuity.

I have selected from his three volumes a hundred examples wherewith to represent Marston as a sonnet-writer. Those who are familiar with his poetry will probably miss some favourites from among these five-score, nor would I assert that I have omitted no noteworthy sonnet. I have, however, done my best not only to choose those which are adequately representative, but those which are most worthy of selection.

It is as a lyrical poet that I consider Marston has most claim upon our attention. Let any reader peruse "The Rose and the Wind," and indeed all its fellows among *Garden Secrets*, "The Old Churchyard of Bonchurch," "Come, Buy," and the half score lyrics grouped together at the end of this book, before he venture to gainsay this opinion.

Perhaps the most remarkable thing about this poet is his early maturity. As already stated, the sonnet called "Desolate" (which I have placed first among the sonnets hereafter) was composed in his fifteenth year: his most noteworthy poem, "A Christmas Vigil," and his finest lyric, "The Rose and the Wind," were written when he was only nineteen. There is, however, a penalty incurred by early maturity, and it would not be wise to assert that Marston escaped aught of forfeiture.

In the stress of literature—a strife not less inevitable, incessant, and remorseless than is every instant being perpetrated in the external world of nature, from the fury for existence in the drop of water to the clashing of those starry spheres whereby our own solar system retains its equipoise —there is no space for superfluity. Only a little can survive, and that little with a difficulty not less than the entry of the rich man into Paradise. Undeniably there is no room for all that Philip Bourke Marston has written, since there is none for many stronger if not sweeter singers than himself: but surely it were wrong, surely it were an uncalled for deprivation of pleasurable moments, to let pass into forgetfulnes the rare and delicate music of a poet who at his best is a singer born, and is of the company of those on Parnassus-hill.

WILLIAM SHARP.

Early Poems.

PRELUDE.

Hear'st thou upon the shore line of thy life,
The beating of this song-tide led by thee,
As by the winds, and moon, is led the sea?
The clashing waves conflicting meet in strife,
Bitter with tears of hopeless love they roll,
And fall, and thunder, between soul and soul.
Strange things are borne upon their foaming heights,
Through wild, grey windy days, and shrieking nights;
O'er rocks and hidden shoals, round beacon lights,
Their foam is blown, till on thy shores at length
They burst, in all the trouble of their strength.

Sad things, O love! upon thy shore they cast—
Waifs from the wreck of that fair dream of joy
With which the winds of Fortune love to toy,
Whereto the waves seem kind, until at last
The tempest burst upon it, in its might;
But through the utter darkness of the night,
The happy haven lights, shone calm and clear

Of that loved land so far, and yet so near.
No voice was left to call, no hand to steer,
It fell before the tempest blind and strong,
To float a wreck upon this tide of song.

This bitter tide, by winds of passion moved:
This stormy tide, that wraps and bears its dead;
This tide, from all strong springs of sorrow fed,
Flowing between my soul and thine beloved;
This tide, that knows no moon by night, by day
No burning sun to flame upon its way;
This passionate, strong tide, whose waste waves roll,
And call from one soul to another soul;
This tide that knows the tempest and the shoal,
The utter darkness, and at best such light
As comes between the day-fall and the night.

Dead hopes, spoiled dreams, sad memories that ache,
Desires whose hopes were vain, poor, sterile prayers;
Such things as these to thee this tide upbears.
Hear where the song waves roar, and where they break,
Let the sharp sound of woe assail thine ears,
Even as his who on some midnight hears
Upon a close, and yet night-hidden strand

The roused sea calling to the silent land,
The strong sea stricken of the storm-wind's hand;
And as he listens, feels himself the pain
Of shipwrecked men, who battle with the main.

Hear it again, in some less stormy mood,
As one who, waking from a dreamless sleep,
Hears the complaining of a moonless deep,
And feels its vast and endless solitude,
With sense of wants untold, his heart oppress;
With terrible strong yearnings to express
All life's untold, unmeasurable woe,
To look past unrevealing stars, and know
Whereto at length, men's prayers and yearnings go.
Once, only once, with purged, and holy eyes,
To see, and know, the promised Paradise.

O love! my land whereto I may not come,
Is not my spirit to thy spirit set?
Hear once, O love! then, if you can, forget,
For when death makes my lips, and your lips, dumb,—
When you have done with pity, I with grief,
When no hope comes to comfort or deceive,
This tide shall flow unchanged upon its way,

And men who catch its beat will surely say,
When comes such love to us in this our day?
What must have been the soul that thus could move
One human spirit to such mighty love?

Small music in its voice this song-tide has,
Not strength enough, perchance, to stir one heart;
No sun, no moon, to it their light impart,
No happy stars above it shining pass;
The summer wots not of it, and no spring,
With winds that sigh, too full of peace to sing,
Can hope to ease it from the tempest's blast;
Between the future and the distant past,
It roars and rolls, its waves fall thick and fast,
Whirled madly by wild winds, and only warm
With pulse and passion of the viewless storm.

EARLY POEMS.

PAST AND FUTURE.

O Love, once more if we
Should meet, and once more stand
Upon the golden strand,
Between the sea and land,
The green land and the sea,

Should we speak of the past,
But two brief years gone by,
When 'neath the summer sky,
Was born what shall not die
While life with me shall last!

Shall I recall that day,
My last of perfect peace,
When, through the branching trees,
The gusty summer breeze
Moved singing on its way!

And far off lay the main !
  But we together stood
  Within that well-loved wood;
  Life looked to me then good,
It looks not so again !

Yes, far off lay the sea,
  And, vaguely and half seen,
  We caught its tender sheen
  Of blue that mixed with green,
As I would mix with thee;

And hold thee for a space
  Within my arms, O sweet,
  Till heart to heart should beat,
  Until our lips should meet,
As in the dear gone days.

A space wherein to sigh,
  With love and bow my head
  Down to your face, and shed
  My soul for you to tread
Beneath your feet, then die !

But strong is fate, O love,
  Who makes, who mars, who ends,
  Whose strength with weakness blends,
  Who joy with sorrow sends—
Just little joy enough

To mock us, crying—lo,
  What might be, and what is!
  Yea often falls the kiss,
  The long-desired bliss,
On lips that nothing know.

O love, what did we say?
  Of course, you cannot tell;
  And I know yet too well
  Each little word that fell
From your lips on that day!

Yea, I shall see till death
  Your face and deep blue eyes,
  And hear the soft short sighs
  That take, with sweet surprise
Of sound, the rapid breath!

Thy lot is sweet for thee,
  Fair, flowery is thy way :
  With thee 'tis always May,
  My life is cold and grey
As any winter sea !

Perchance you may recall
  That mute warm summer's night,
  When with the moon's clear light
  The sea was calm and bright,
And no wind was at all !

And hardly could the deep
  Get strength to kiss the strand,
  The sea-wet shining sand ;
  A spell lay on the land
As of great love and sleep !

Still, love, my sad sight sees,
  As in the days that were,
  Your eyes that would not spare,
  And light of golden hair
As flame blown by a breeze !

Oh, sound of vanished feet,
  Oh, sad remembering
  In winter of the spring!
  My lips now only sing
Sad songs, and no more sweet!

I shall live on and see
  Fresh people and fresh days,
  But none the reason trace
  Why one name of one place
Is more than tune to me!

But when you hear the name,
  The reason you may find.
  O fair land left behind!
  O sea of summer, blind
With light of summer flame!

Yea, love! no more may we
  Together walk or stand
  Upon the golden strand,
  Between the sea and land,
The green land and the sea!

A CHRISTMAS VIGIL.

ROUND the vast city draws the twilight gray;
I know men say,
This evening is the eve of Christmas Day,
But what has Christmas time to do with me,
Who live a shameful life out shamelessly?
A creature now that doth not even yearn
From sin to turn;
Too blind perchance it may be to discern
God's mighty mercy, and the boundless love
That all paid, praying preachers tell us of.

Here he lies dead, with whom my shame began,
This is the man!
Through whom my life to such dishonour ran.
He was the snare in which my soul was caught;
Oh, the sweet ways wherein for love he wrought.
Yet God, not *he*, my wrath of soul shall bear,
God set the snare!

God made him lustful, and God made me fair.
O God! were not his kisses more to me
Than Christians' hopes of immortality?

O lovely, wasted fingers, lithe and long,
So kind and strong;
O lips! wherein all laughter was a song,
All song as laughter. O the cold, calm face,
The speechless marble mouth, that had such ways
Of singing, that for very joy of it,
My heart would beat
Almost as loud as when our lips would meet,
And all love's passion, hotter for its shame,
Set panting mouths and thirsting eyes on flame.

Thus, would I part this hair back from the brow;
But look you now,
What thing is left for me, save this, to bow
Myself unto him, as in days gone by,
To stretch myself beside him, and to die;
To crush my burning, aching lips on his,
In one long kiss;
To know how cold and strange a thing death is?
His lips are cold, but my lips are so hot,
That all death's fearful coldness chills them not.

Fast falls the night, and down the iron street,
Loud ring the feet
Of happy people, who pass on to meet
Fair sights of home ; I hear the roll and roar
Of traffic, like a sea upon a shore.
One dying candle's pallid light is shed
Upon the bed
Whereon is laid my beautiful, cold dead,—
Mine, altogether mine, for two brief days !
Are not these hands his hands ; this face his face ?

And now I can recall the time gone by,
The pure fresh sky
Of spring, 'neath which we first met, he and I,
The smell of rainy fields in early spring,
The song of thrushes, and the glimmering
Of rain-drenched leaves by sudden sun made bright,
The tender light
Of peaceful evening, and the saintly night.
Sweet still the scent of roses ; only this,
They had a perfume then which now I miss.

Yea, too, I can recall the night wherein
Did first begin
The joy of that intoxicating sin.

Late was the day in April, gray and still,
Too faint to gladden, and too mild to chill;
Hot lay upon my lips the last night's kiss,
The first of his;
I wandered blindly between shame and bliss;
And, yearning, hung all day about the lane,
Where, in the evening, he should come again.

Now, when the time of the sun's setting came,
The sky caught flame;
For all the sun, which as an empty name
Had been that day, then rent the leaden veil
And flashed out sharp, 'twixt watery clouds, and pale,
Then, suddenly, a stormy wind upsprang,
That shrieked and sang;
Around the reeling tree-tops, loud it rang,
And all was dappled blue, and faint, fresh gold,
Lovely, and virgin; wild, and sweet, and cold.

Then through the wind I heard his voice ring out,
And half in doubt,
Trembling and glad, I turned, and looked about,
And saw him standing in my downward way,
Full in the splendour of the dying day.

Silent I stood a space, and then at last
Strong arms were cast
About me, and his burning spirit passed
Into my spirit, till the twain as one
Shone out together under passion's sun.

I felt that joy unnameable was near;
A great sweet fear
Fell all around me, and no thing was clear
To me save this,—that in his arms I lay,
And felt his kisses burn my soul away.
I heard the wild wind singing in my hair,
And saw the fair
Green branches tossing in the stormy air;
And, through the failing light, I heard a voice
That cried, "O soul, at least this night rejoice!'

Ah me! the shameless, limitless delight
Of that spring night!
The magic ways wherein, 'twixt dusk and light,
I wandered, dazed and faint with joy's excess—
Ah, God! what human creature shall express
That night's dear joy, the long thirst quenched at last,
All shame outcast,

The haven entered, and the tempest passed?
O shameful, sacred night, whereby alone
I bear with life till life's last day be done!

But when the feverish night had passed away,
And faint, and grey,
On wet, chill April fields calm broke the day,
I rose, and in an altered world had part;
Love, marred by shame, lay bitter at my heart.
Through all my daily rounds that day I went,
Till day was spent;
And with the night once more came sweet content,
And joy that shut out every thought of shame,
And made all infamy an empty name.

Then quickly came the waste, gold, summer days,
The blinding blaze
Of burning sunlight, and the sultry ways
Of breathless nights, wherein the moon seemed strange,
And with the scent of roses came the change;
Yea, when, as naked blades sharp-edged and bright,
'Neath blasting light,

Sharp flashed the streams ; when every coming night,
Solemn with moonlight, or with stars thrilled through,
Or quite unlit but passionately blue,

Were sweet as rest—'mid song, and scent, and flame,
To me there came
The sense of loss, and bitterness of shame.
Surely between his kisses he had said,
'O love ! before the summer time has fled,
I will return, and thou with me shalt come
To a fair home.'
My kisses answered, for my voice was dumb.
Ah, God ! those terrible June days, wherein
No rapture came to hush the voice of sin.

O sickening perfume of those summer days !
O tree-girt ways
Wherein we wandered ! O the happy place
Where first I burst on love, and love on me !
O sleepless nights when tears fell bitterly !
So died the Summer ; and the Autumn sweet,
With languid feet ;

And recollections of the by-gone heat
Came down to us ; but still he came no more,
And then I knew my destiny was sure.

I know not how, at length, when hope was gone,
                                        And shame had grown
Too sharp a thing to be endured alone,
I left the peaceful country far behind,
And to the mighty city came to find
Some opiate for pain, and found it, too.
                                        Fresh passions grew
Within me : and a little while I knew
The bitter joys that set the blood on flame :
So grief slays joy, and wretchedness slays shame.

But still, through every feverish night and day,
                                        The old love lay
Hot at my heart, though he had gone his way,
As I had mine : sometimes of him I heard,
And how the world was by his spirit stirred.
Then came the news, how he lay dying here !
                                        I shed no tear,
I only felt the time at length was near,
When meeting I should see his face again,
And feel, through all, I had not lived in vain.

And now it is two nights ago, since first
With eyes athirst
To see his face, resolved to know the worst,
I came in here, and stood beside his bed :
No look he gave me, and no word he said ;
But I said, bowing down, and speaking low—
'Two years ago,
You slew my honour, and I come here now
To tell you, whether yet you die or live,
Lost as I am, I love you, and forgive.'

He turned, and then I knew that he would speak ;
Against my cheek
Hot beat the blood, I stood there dazed and weak ;
He said—'O face and voice that I remember,
'Twas July then, and now it is December ;
Poor dove ! that all God's hawks for prey have got.
Ah me ! how hot
This fever burns, and she remembers not
The ways of love wherein last June we trod !
They work their will, this woman and her God.'

Thus, as towards ending of his speech he drew,
I only knew
Some other bitter mem'ry had come through

His thoughts of me, and set his soul adrift :
Then, as he backward fell, I saw him lift
Bright hollow eyes unto the wall, whereon
A picture shone—
A picture now that from the wall has gone;
A portrait of a woman strange as fair,
With calm grey eyes, and fitful gold of hair.

The pale calm face, immovable and sad,
Such beauty had,
As well might make by love a strong man mad.
The long sweet hands upon her breast were laid,
The full throat just a little back was swayed,
Its firm white beauty better to expose;
The mouth kept close
The spirit's secrets of all joys and woes ;
So calm and still he lay, I thought he slept,
Till, bending nearer down, I knew he wept.

And then he said, as one who speaks in dreams,
'O face that gleams
Upon me when in sleep my spirit seems
To walk with thine, O long-loved love, O sweet,
O vanished eyes, O unreturning feet !

'O heart that all the tempest of my love
Could no way move!
O death, is not the end now sharp enough—
To love her, and to lose her, and to die,
While she knows not how life is going by?

'Could she know all I think she would arise,
And let her eyes,
Wherein the very calm of heaven lies,
Fall on my face; yea, too, I do believe
So sweet her sweet soul is that she would grieve
A little space, in silence sitting here,
To see draw near
Death's sea o'er which no light and land appear;
Yea, too, with words and touches she might make
The death-ward path smile as a flowering brake.'

Then all his love came on him, and he cried,—
'O death! divide
My soul from thought of hers; O darkness! hide
The passionless cold face and speechless mouth
By mine unkissed that waste my soul with drought!
O love, and must I die unkissed by thee?
What man shall be

The chosen one to come 'twixt thee and me?'
Then forth into the air he stretched his hand,
As one who, drowning, strives to reach the land.

Upon his brow a trembling hand I laid,
And tearless said,—
'Lie down and rest.' Then, as the rain is shed
When awful thunder-storms break up the heat,
My kisses on his lips and eyelids beat,
My fingers met and closed within his hair,
He was so fair;
And, like the unhoped granting of a prayer,
Such prayers as dying men for life must pray,
At length upon my hand his kisses lay.

Then by him, bowed with all my love, I fell,
And cried, ''Tis well,
Live yet, and in thy presence let me dwell.'
He smiled, and said, 'O tender hands and kind,
O lovely worshipped hands that now I find
So sweet, so sweet! O love, that bringest bliss,
What joy is this
To gain at last the heaven of thy kiss?'
And then he turned himself, gave thanks and sighed,
Nor spake again; and in the dawn he died.

My lips sealed up his eyes, my hands were spread
Beneath his head.
I stretched the lovely limbs upon the bed,
Folded the wasted hands upon the breast;
As there he lay in calm and frozen rest,
The drawn and rigid lips looked cold and stern,
That seemed to spurn
All joys and griefs; no soul was left to yearn
Within the hollow, dreamless, lampless eyes,
Whose death-look said the dead soul shall not rise.

I know not whether I did wrong or right,
But in the night
I came into his room, and raised the light
Unto the pictured face upon the wall
That looked on his, and was not moved at all;
I took it down, the face indeed was fair;
But, standing there,
I spurned it with my foot as God spurns prayer,
And lacking strength, not will, to spoil the face,
I cast it forth where none might know its grace.

And yet I think sometimes if he could know,
Loving her so,
As men, O God, can love and bear with woe,

He might be angry for the face downcast,
And for it come to hate me at the last ;
But now the heavy tread upon the stair
Of men who bear
Some strange thing up : they come, they will not spare.
O God ! they come, and now the door goes back ;
They smell of death, the thing they bear is black.

SIR LAUNCELOT'S SONG TO GUENEVERE.

SHE is fresh and she is bright,
Joyous as the morning light;
Tender as a summer night,
Wherein men lose their souls for bliss,
And airs come wafted like a kiss
From crimson lips of Guenevere.
Who so stately, who so fair
As my own love, Guenevere?

When were ever seen such eyes,
Where the love-light faints and flies?
Such a crimson paradise
As her sweet mouth rife with love
Murmuring secret joys thereof?
Droop above me, Guenevere!
Who has lips, and eyes, and hair
Like thine own, my Guenevere?

When the sun had left the west,
With head upon her fair white breast,
Oft at night times would I rest,
While, the listening space along,

Poured the music of her song
That told the love of Guenevere.
What in witchery may compare
With the voice of Guenevere?

Who has ever seen such feet,
Round which jewelled sandals meet,
Sweetly indolent or fleet
As love prompts or pleasure stays?
Love shines royal in the face
Of my royal Guenevere.
Love that doth a sceptre bear
Yields it to my Guenevere.

Thrills her touch through pulse and vein,
Flooding each with rapturous pain
That of its excess doth wane;
Moves she as a laden vine
That doth rise or now decline
As the love-gust sweeps by her;
Who is various, who is fair
As my own love, Guenevere?

La Belle Iseult is fair, we know;
Her mouth a rose, her bosom snow;
Such charms for other men may blow,
Their beauties may, for my will, pass

Like their own semblance in a glass,
If they leave but Guenevere.
Who has brows so fit to wear
Love's crown as my Guenevere?

Morgan le Fay is fair and wise,
With strange words in her lips and eyes,
That read the secrets of the skies;
She's too weird, too grave for me,
Too like a tranced summer sea.
Changeful is my Guenevere;
Whom shall mortal eyes compare
In each change with Guenevere?

AFTER MANY DAYS.

In autumn's silent twilight, sad and sweet,
O love, no longer mine, alone I stand;
Listening, I seem to hear dear phantom feet
Pass by me down the golden wave-worn strand:
I think of things that were and things that be,
I hear the soft low ripples of the sea
That to my thoughts responsive music beat.

My heart is very sad to-night and chill,
But hushed in awe, as his who turns and feels
A mournful rapture through his being thrill,
When music, sweet and slumb'rous, softly steals
Down the deep calm of some cathedral nave;
Then swells and throbs and breaks as does a wave,
And slowly ebbs, and all again is still.

And is it only five years since, O love,
That we in this old place stood side by side
Where in the twilight once again I move?
Is this the same shore washed by the same tide?

My heart recalls the past a little space,
The sweet and the irrevocable days ;
I knew not then how bitter life might prove.

I loved you then, and shall love till I die ;
Your way of life is fair, it should be so,
And I am glad, though in dark years gone by
Hard thoughts of you I had ; but now I know
A fairer and a softer path was meet
For treading of your dainty maiden feet :
Your life must blossom 'neath a summer sky.

The twilight, like a sleep, creeps on the day,
And like dark dreams the night creeps on that sleep ;
If you should come again in the old way
And look from pensive tender eyes and deep
Upon me, as you looked in days of old—
If my hand should again of yours take hold,
How should I feel, and what thing should I say ?

Ah, sweet days flown shall never come again ;
That happy summer time shall not return
When we two stood beside this peaceful main,
And saw at eve the rising billows yearn

With passion to the moon, and heard afar,
Across the waves, and 'neath the first warm star,
From ships at sea some sweet remembered strain.

I can recall the day when first we met,
And how the burning summer sunlight fell
Across the sea; nor, love, do I forget
How, underneath that summer noontide spell,
We saw afar the white-sailed vessels glide
As phantom ships upon a waveless tide,
Whose shining calm no breezes come to fret.

And shall I blame you, sweet, because you chose
A softer path of life than mine could be?
I keep our secret here, and no man knows
What passed five years ago 'twixt you and me—
Two loves begotten at the self-same time,
When that gold summer tide was in its prime:
One love lives yet, and one died with the rose.

I work and live and take my part in things,
And so my life goes on from day to day;
Fruitless the summers, seedless all the springs,
To him who feels December one with May:

The night is not more dreary than the sun,
Not sadder is the twilight, dim and dun,
Than dawn that, still returning, shines and sings.

Fed with wet scent of hills, through growing shades,
To the white water's edge the wind moans down;
The lapping tide steals on, while daylight fades,
And fills the caves with shells and seaweed brown.
Ah, wild sea-beaten coast, more dear to me
Than fairest scenes of that fair land could be
Where warm Italian suns steep happy glades!

Farewell, familiar scene, for I ascend
The jagged path that led me to the shore;
Farewell to cliff, cave, inlet—each a friend;
My parting steps shall visit ye no more:
Dear are ye all where soft light steals through gloom,
Here had my joy its birth—here found its tomb—
Here love began, and here one love had end.

OUT OF EDEN.

Again the summer comes, and all is fair ;
A sea of tender blue, the sky o'erhead
Stretches its peace ; the roses white and red,
Through the deep silence of the trancéd air,
In a mute ecstasy of love declare
Their souls in perfume, while their leaves are fed
With dew and moonlight that fall softly shed
Like slumber on pure eyelids unaware.

O wasted affluence of scent and light !
Each gust of fragrance smites me tauntingly ;
Yon placid stars have rankling shafts for me ;
My great despair, by its own fatal might,
Converts to pain the loveliness of night.
Ah, would I could from all this beauty flee,
And, 'neath some grey sky on a cheerless sea,
Let drift a life that cannot end aright.

Vain flower of fame from which is gone the scent,
Vain crown no longer glorious in mine eyes,
Vain hopes at which, years back, my joy would rise
Like melody within an instrument

When skilled hands touch the strings. All now is spent
And what is gained? Lo, I have gained my prize,
And here neglected at my feet it lies;
It meant so much: I now ask what it meant.

For thee, lost love, I shall not see again;
The pale sad beauty of thy tender face,
Once lamp and light of this now starless place,
Comes to me in my dreams, and I am fain
To hold thee in my arms, and so retain
Thy phantom form in one long wild embrace:
A flush illumes the features of dead days,
But fades before the lights in heaven wane.

I am as one who, in a festive hall
Ablaze with glow of flowers and cresset fires,
Hears from a hundred joy-begetting lyres
A storm of music roll from wall to wall,
Yet feels no joy upon his spirit fall,
For all the while his wandering heart desires
One small sweet waif of sound those pealing quires
May scorn—may drown, but never can recall.

Yea, seem I like that fabled king of old
Who gained his wish, and woke one morn—and lo!

With gold his bed and chamber were aglow,
  And when his glad arms did his child enfold,
  He clasped but to his heart a form of gold—
Gold roses in her breast, no more of snow,
Gold hair upon her gold and polished brow,
  Hard, bright the hands of which his hands took
    hold.

  But from her golden trance he saw her wake,
Saw life and bloom return to all the flowers;
Green grew again and fresh the wind-stirred bowers,
  And from its golden frost was freed the lake;
  But, though I drain my heart for *my* love's sake,
She will not come to make my waste of hours
Fruitful as earth beneath warm sun and showers,
  Nor quick with scent *my* scentless roses make.

  Dear soul, to-night our wedding-night had been,
And death has come to you and fame to me;
The summer's breath makes music in the tree,
  Its kiss with over-love has charred the green,
  Through quivering boughs I catch night's starry
    sheen,
A sense of unborn music seems to be
In air and moonlight falling tenderly,
  And yet I draw no sweetness from the scene.

O love, sweet love, my first, my only love,
How can I find the flowering meadows sweet
That no more feel the kisses of your feet !
O silent heart that grief no more can move.
O loved and loving lips, whereto mine clove
Till hope, long stanch, with thy heart's muffled beat
Furled his lorn flag and made his last retreat,
And all was void below, and dark above.

Pale form, they should have clothed thee like a bride,
Have twined a bridal chaplet round thy head,
And decked thy cold grave as a marriage-bed ;
For, though the envious darkness do thee hide,
I still shall find thee, sweet, and by thy side
Lie peaceful down while hands and lips shall wed,
And winds, attuned to lays of love we said,
Float o'er the stillness where we twain abide.

But now the gulf between us, love, is deep :
I labour yet a little in the fight,
And bear the outrage of the joyous light,
I toil by day, and in the night I sleep,
And then my heart gets ease, for I can weep ;
But you in starless, songless depths of night,
With dreamless slumber shed upon your sight,
Rest where none need to sow, or care to reap.

A VISION.

LYING between two sleeps, I did behold
  A vision strange, and terrible, and sad,
    Which seemed to me the key
    That opened all my wards of destiny.
Now listen, all who will, while I unfold
  The vision that I had.

Beside my bed I saw a man's form stand;
  His brows were wasted as by wasting fire,
    Madness was in his gaze,
    Pain, with fierce lips, fed on his haggard face,
A gleaming serpent twined about his hand,
  Pale victim of desire!

A strange and vivid wreath entwined his head—
  The myrtle green, the poppy, and the rose;
    Across his bare white feet
    Did snakes again for fiery sandals meet;
With blood the parched and pallid lips were red
  That o'er his pangs did close.

Upon his limbs a fiery garment shone;
At length, with lips unlocked, I heard him cry,—
'Oh, pain of great delight,
Be the sky fair with day or black with night,
'Tis all one thing with me, by sin led on
To where no tortures die!'

Dead, lying at his feet, I then did see
The figure of a boy still pure and fair;
And by his side one knelt
Whose loveliness through every sense did melt,
As through the soul melts some wild melody:
Her supple limbs were bare.

Sea-blossoms quivered in her dazzling breast,
Roses and poppies round her brows did twine,
About her body burned
Splendour of crimson fire; to me she turned,
Unto my sight the goddess stood confest,
Daughter of blood and brine!

Great Aphrodite gazed upon me there:
Then I looked down upon the boy, and lo,

His throat with blood was red ;
And now her fingers clutched the white throat dead.
I know not if he uttered any prayer,
Or when she dealt the blow.

And then I saw, with wonder and great fear,
The man's face, in a cold and death-set likeness,
Upon the boy's face sweet,
His eyes, his hair, his very hands and feet ;
Their souls seemed far apart as sphere from sphere,
Or blood from snow's cold whiteness.

And as I gazed a space with straining eyes,
I saw the vision fading through the gloom ;
And, as it fainter grew,
I heard, the thick and growing darkness through,
Fierce laughter, weary wails, then short, sad sighs—
Then silence like the tomb.

TO A CHILD.

I KISS you, dear, and very sweet is this,
To feel you are not tainted by my kiss ;
Cling with your warm soft arms about me so,
Give me one small sweet kiss and murmur low,
In speech as sweet as broken music is.

How long shall God my Lily darling give
Untainted by the shrieking world to live,
I cannot tell ; but this my wish shall be,
Longer at least than God has given me,
But still be glad ; as yet, you need not grieve.

There, see, I put the hair back from your face,
And if my lips in kissing should displace
Your sunny hair, you will but laugh, my child,
A babbling silver laugh and undefiled.
God keep it so, through the all-ruling days.

But, I, who in the darkness sit alone,
With heart that, once rebellious, now has grown
  Too weak to strive with foes that smite unseen,
  Will only ask you once your head to lean
Upon a heart where grief has made his throne.

I will not tell you of the things I know,
I cannot bar the path that you must go ;
  God's bitter lesson must be learnt by all,
  But living, I will listen to your call,
And stretch to you a hand that you may know.

You feel the wind against you as you run,
And love its strength, and revel in the sun ;
  So once did I, and but for this last blow,
  Of which none know save me, so might I now ;
But now for me the light of life is done.

These little hands that lose themselves in mine,
May some day haply in a man's hair twine
  While 'neath their touch his heart shall palpitate,
  Then shall this soul with triumph be elate
And mix sharp poison in a maddening wine.

But see you keep your lips from tasting, sweet,
For it begets within us such a heat,
  As cooling waters never can allay.
  We see, through mists of blood and tears, the day,
Until we sicken for the nightfall's feet.

There, there, you're weary, and I let you go,
But this kiss, softer than a flake of snow,
  I will remember when alone I stand.
  I wonder will you ever understand
The reason why I loved and kissed you so.

THE LAST REVEL.

So now our one month's love is done.
  Good-bye, my love ! good-bye !
Before to-morrow's burning sun
  Flames golden in the sky,
We shall be far apart, my sweet,
No more, no more to meet.

How well I know this chamber, dear,
  A blaze of mirrors tall ;
The lattice too, wherethrough we hear
  The sighing water fall
Upon the steps that from the sea
Lead up, my love, to thee.

Lo ! how the softened lamp-light rests
  Upon your gleaming hair ;
Upon your splendid foam-white breasts,
  Bright shoulders curved and bare.
Let's fill once more the goblet up,
And kiss across the cup.

How hushed the great warm heavens are;
  The sultry moonlight lies
Upon the sea, and one vast star
  Possesses all the skies.
Down the dim water streets we see
The boats glide dreamily.

Sing me again the song I heard
  You sing that first sweet night,
When, to my senses stained and blurred,
  O'er wastes of glaring light,
In all the glory of the song,
Your voice came clear and strong.

But first from instruments there stole
  Strange music, soft and low,
I felt through all my wearied soul
  The gentle music flow:
And in the tender harmonies
My heart lay faint with peace.

And when again you sing that song,
  And all men cry your name,
Some thought of me may lurk among
  The thoughts of gold and fame;
You may perchance recall this night,
And all our past delight.

You say you will remember well;
  The speech sounds sweet and smooth,
And though I know for gold you sell
  The kisses of your mouth,
Your eyes' keen fires, your hair's bright hue,
Yet still it may be true.

And so you thought me cold at first,
  My calm eyes chilled your bliss;
But when you saw my lips athirst
  To taste your longed-for kiss,
You found me better, did you not?
Girls like a man's blood hot.

But when the passion fades away,
  The chill comes back, you think;
'Strange was that Englishman,' you'll say;
  'He kissed, and he could drink,
And in the middle of a feast
Be solemn as a priest.'

And did it never strike you, love,
  That in his heart might be,
That which your kiss was not enough
  To banish utterly;
A thought he could not quite shut out,
Yet could not speak about?

How if grief snared him in his land,
  And tracked him o'er the sea?
A grief from whose relentless hand
  He never might get free;
A grief that slept not in the night,
But murdered all delight.

A grief, which, when you sang your best,
  Outsang you with its voice,
Chanting in pain, and long unrest,
  Its dirge for buried joys;
A sadder song than ever man
Sang since the world began.

I do not say it is so, mind,
  Only, if so it be,
You might perchance some reason find
  To wonder less at me;
But vain to speak to you of this,
Who sell, not give, love's kiss.

I take you in my arms again;
  O shoulders bright and smooth,
Soft throat whereon my kisses rain,
  Keen eyes and glowing mouth;
Once more I feel a strong blood yearn
Within my veins, and burn.

What is the gift you give to me,
  And what the gift I give?
I hold the right your face to see
  As long as I shall live,
And you this bracelet like a snake,
To wear a day—and break.

A MEDLEY.

A LILY are you? such you seem,
  A lily brimmed with dew and scent;
With languid, listless leaves that gleam,
  By heat made sweetly indolent,
  While all the sky with love is hot,
  Such love as Earth remembers not
When June is but a lovely dream.

You seem in soul a panther bright,
  With velvet paws, but made to slay;
A lily laughing in the light,
  A panther seeking after prey:
  A panther fair, with noiseless tread,
  A lily, with bowed stem, and head,
Lapped in the loveliness of night.

So very fair, the smallest thing
  On which you look at once looks fair;
And but to hear you play and sing,
  Would make with envy Orpheus swear.

Forgive me, if I leave a space,
The lily and the panther phase,
Your touch, and voice remembering.

To be of all men's hearts the Queen
Is surely, lady, good enough;
Your looks are sweet, your words are keen,
To first exalt, then humble love.
'Tis better far to worship thee
Than Venus, old world deity,
Whose loveliness is praised unseen.

And men years hence shall know you as
One lily-formed and panther-souled,
The gods themselves did quite surpass
Your spirit and your form to mould.
They made you as a poet makes
His best rhyme when his hand so shakes
It scarce can hold the pen or glass.

More clear than notes of music be
Your voice, in no two words the same;
A sudden burst of melody
To glorify with sound a name?
With ear and eye assailed at once,
Against such fatal needle-guns
The man who would be safe must flee.

A poem with a double sense,
  A joy, a grief, a tiger-lily,
With images I now dispense;
  My flower I leave in the wild nook hilly,
  In the forest the panther fleet,
  My song is kneeling at your feet,
Give it one smile for recompense.

A curious medley is this verse
  Of lilies, poets, panthers, guns,
I may sing better or sing worse,
  But no more thus my swift verse runs;
  For soon I write a song most fit
  To be in ladies' albums writ
And read by all the universe.

BEFORE BATTLE.

HERE in this place, where none can see,
  Lean out your throat, and let us kiss;
Who knows, to-morrow I may be
  As far from any joy like this,
As is my own sèa-beaten strand
                From this fair land.

She put the hair back from her face,
  And kissed him on his eager mouth;
Her kiss was warm, and long her gaze,
  He felt the passion of his youth
Burn fierce through every thrilling vein,
                Till it was pain.

He filled for her a cup of wine,
  The sparkling wine as red as blood,
She quickly drank, and for a sign
  He kissed its edge, as saints the rood,
Before Death plucks their souls away,
                Too faint to pray.

He said, 'O love, the wine is sweet,
  But, sweet, thy kiss is sweeter still!'
She flushed, with sudden joy and heat,
  She said, 'O love, then take thy fill
Of both these things, for both thine are,
      Before the war.'

Another cup of wine he quaffed,
  Then in his arms her form he pressed,
He murmured low; she sighed and laughed,
  And they clung fiercely breast to breast:
While all her hair fell round his face,
      Her love to grace.

She thrilled with passion, till her lips
  Could nothing do, but kiss and cleave,
Their souls were like sea-driven ships;
  He felt her swelling bosom heave;
His lips her lips with kisses flaked,
      Till both lips ached.

His face above her fair, flushed face,
  Now seemed a thing to wonder on;
Her soul was ravished by his gaze,
  Her warm, wet eye-lids shook and shone,
Till, leaning back, for pure delight,
      She laughed outright.

He wrung her long sweet fingers out,
  He strained the passion at her mouth,
Her hair was all his face about,
  O life to life! O youth to youth!
O sea of joy, whose foam is fire!
                    O great desire!

But, suddenly, a sharp shrill sound
  Cut like a sword their dear delight;
Once more his arms about her wound,
  They felt their pulses beat and smite.
At last he said, in accents low,
                    'The foe! the foe!'

Then quickly from her arms he sprang;
  For all the night-black winding street
With clash of deadly weapons rang,
  And sudden storm of passing feet;
She heard the thunder of the drum.
                    Her lips grew dumb.

'O one night's love! Good-bye!' he said,
  And kissed her on the lips, and passed.
She heard his quick, departing tread,
  She saw the torches glare at last,
She saw the street grow light as day,
                    And swooned away.

An hour afterwards, or more,
With stormy music, loud and long,
With light behind, and light before,
The men marched down, an armèd throng:
And as they passed, he saw her light
Still burning bright.

She from her chamber-window leant,
Deep down into the street to gaze;
Her head upon her hands was bent:
He looked, but could not see her face;
But still he thought, through sound and flame,
She cried his name.

She watched the torches fade away,
She listened till the street grew still,
Then back upon her bed she lay,
Of her own thoughts to drink her fill;
And afterwards, when others wept,
She only slept.

Next night she revelled in the dance,
She quaffed her wine, she sang her song;
While he, with soldier's eyes askance,
And heart with lust of slaying strong,
Leaped laughing into battle's hell,
And struck and fell!

WAITING.

WHEN shall I see that land where I would tread,
That shrine where I would fain bow knee and head?
In autumn—ere the autumn pass, I said;
In winter—ere the winter time is sped,
In spring—ere yet spring's fair sweet feet are fled,
In summer—ere the summer time is shed—
And now I say, perchance when I am dead.

IN GRIEF.

WITH thee so vanished our life's light has flown,
A sudden night has fallen on the day—
A cheerless, moonless night with no white way
Of stars that lead to lands of men unknown.
A night wherein the winds of grief are loud,
A night made black with sorrow as a cloud,
A night that wraps its darkness as a shroud
Around a world now sad, and cold, and gray.

God fashioned thee and gave thy spirit birth
To ease a little our sore load of pain;
More sweet to us thy love was than the rain
Is after long, hot days to burnt-up earth.
Thou wert a refuge in a stormy deep,
From thee there flowed a peace like conscious sleep.
I will not sow sweet things who may not reap,
I will not strive who nothing here may gain.

As is to one within his dungeon's gloom
  A sudden burst of music and of light,
  Cleaving the darkness, trancing ear and sight,
Making resplendent what is still his tomb;
    So living to my prisoned soul thou wert;
    Now all once more is dark about my heart,
    No light, nor any sound its depth shall part,
  And there shall be no daybreak to this night.

Now all is done; no more is left to do:
  A space we stood together on life's shore
  Waving weak hands to those who went before;
Thou knowest now if heavenly skies are blue,
    Thou knowest if the after world is sweet,
    Dost thou tread light or darkness 'neath thy feet?
    When with weak hands upon the gate we beat
  Will it be opened, or closed evermore?

And shall we meet with lips that yearn to kiss,
  Meet soul to soul as face to face on earth?
  And shall there be an end of death and dearth,
Yea, shall there be a harvest time of bliss,
    And shall we stand together side by side
    Never again to sorrow or divide?
    And shall at length our hearts be satisfied
  Full of the wonder of the second birth?

Shall this life past be as a dream outdreamed,
The ghastly fancy of a fevered brain?
Shall we at all remember the old pain,
So great it past all human bearing seemed?
If angels tell us of that mournful time,
Will it then sound but as an empty rhyme
Made by a boy in some forgotten clime?
Ah, shall we say we have not lived in vain?

Shall we stand up before the face of God,
Stand up and sing a loud, glad song of praise,
And bless him for the sorrow of our days,
And kiss with pure cold lips the burning rod
Wherewith he hath so stricken us that we
Might come at length within his home to be,
Laid in the light of his divinity,
First blinded by the glory of his face?

Oh, strange and unseen land whereto we come,
Are thy shores shores of day or shores of night?
As near we draw shall we indeed see light,
And shall we hear, through lessening wind and foam,
The voice of her we love come from the land,
And, looking shorewards, shall we see her stand
Girt round with glory on a peaceful strand,
Smiling to see our dark skiff heave in sight?

I cannot know; there is no man who knows;
 We are and we are not, and that is all
 The knowledge which to any may befall:
We know not life's beginning nor life's close,
  'Twixt dawn and twilight shine the sunny hours
  Wherein some hands plucked thorns and some hands flowers,
  'Twixt light and shade are shed the sudden showers;
 Yet night shall cover earth as with a pall.

Sadder than all thou art, O song of mine,
 Because thou callest vainly on her name,
 Because thou fain wouldst rise and sudden flame
Before God's face and her face most divine,
  And tell her of the bitter grief we feel,
  And pray her by some sweet sign to reveal
  The land which God and darkness so conceal—
Say where our sorrows lead and whence they came.

O saddest of sad songs by sad lips sung,
 Fresh hopes may rise, fresh passions snakelike hiss,
 Or fresh illusions find fresh rods to kiss;
But joy is fleet and memory is long.

And on the fair sweet reaches of the past,
Lovely and still, for evermore is cast
A sad and sacred light which shall outlast
The fierce and short-lived glare of summer bliss.

Alas, poor song, all singing is in vain,
What thing more sad is left for thee to say?
Oh, weary time of life and weary way,
Can dead souls rise or gone joys come again?
Now by the hand of sorrow are we led,
Though sweet things come, they come as joys born dead;
Let us arise, go hence, for all is said,
And we must bide the breaking of the day.

Poems from "All in All."

POEMS FROM "ALL IN ALL."

INSEPARABLE.

When I and thou are dead, my dear,
The earth above us lain,
When we no more in autumn hear
The fall of leaves and rain,
Or round the snow-enshrouded year
The midnight winds complain.

When we no more in green mid-spring,
Its sights and sounds may mind;
The warm wet leaves set quivering
With touches of the wind,
The birds at morn, and birds that sing,
When day is left behind.

When over all the moonlight lies,
Intensely bright and still;

When some meandering brooklet sighs,
At parting from its hill ;
And scents from voiceless gardens rise,
The peaceful air to fill.

When we no more through summer light
The deep, dim woods discern,
Nor hear the nightingales at night,
In vehement singing, yearn
To stars and moon, that, dumb and bright,
In nightly vigil burn.

When smiles, and hopes, and joys, and fears,
And words that lovers say ;
And sighs of love, and passionate tears
Are lost to us for aye,
What thing of all our love appears,
In cold and coffin'd clay ?

When all their kisses, sweet and close,
Our lips shall quite forget ;
When, where the day upon us rose,
The day shall rise and set,
While we for love's sublime repose
Shall have not one regret ;—

Oh, this true comfort is, I think,
  That, be death near or far,
When we have crossed the fatal brink,
  And found nor moon nor star—
To know not when in death we sink,
  The lifeless things we are.

Yet one thought is, I deem, more kind,
  That when we sleep so well,
On memories that we leave behind,
  When kindred spirits dwell,
My name to thine, in words they'll bind,
  Of love inseparable.

IN THE JUNE TWILIGHT.

In the June twilight, starless and profound,
She sits : and of the twilight seems a part.
No birds sing now, nor is there any sound
Of wind among the leaves ; faintly you hear
The distant beating of the city's heart :
It doth not break the spell nor vex the ear,
But seems the silence yet to make more deep,
As though some giant whispered in his sleep.
Sometimes from little gardens lying round,
A voice calls through the evening ; or you catch
The sound of opening windows, or a latch
Rais'd stealthily beneath, by those who keep
Love's trists, that often are too bitter found.
And lo ! one sits beside her ; does she know
How the least tone of hers, the slightest noise
Of soft, stirr'd raiment sets his heart aglow ?
Yea, does she see how all the soul of him
Yearns to her in his look and in his voice ?
Their faces in the falling light are dim ;
And now to ease his heart a little space,

He tells her songs, that Love, with sovereign grace,
Has given him to sing of her; that so,
When Time, grown weary, casts his soul away
As a thing wholly done with, men shall say—
"How this man loved, and she his verses praise:
Such women come not twice God's grace to show."

And now he ceases; and the common things
Of outer life go on: she does not move,
Her soul is full of mystic whisperings.
Is this heart hers, to do with as she wills?
But men as well as women can feign love,
Or deem *that* love which time too quickly kills.
But has she kindled in this man the fire
That only with his being can expire?
And starts he, when she looks at him, and springs
The violent blood through each dilating vein
When her hand touches his? can love be pain?
Can love unloving hearts with love inspire,
And is her love the heaven of which he sings?

FIRST KNOWLEDGE.

WHEN in sad sweetness and delicious dole
Love whispered her, "Thou lovest," did she start,
Confronted with that knowledge in her heart?
Or, did she pause to comprehend the whole
Deep meaning of Love's speech, and no word say?
As some musician who, about to play
The sweetest tune his cunning can essay,
Sits with still hands among the harp-chords lain,
Seeming to hearken with his heart and brain
Part of the music, ere it breaks and springs
From out the thrill'd, expectant, shuddering strings.

Did she think over love, of lovers dead,
And say, "Is such our love?" Did she recall
His steadfast look, his bitter sighs, and all
Sad words that at their parting he had said,
Not thinking he might ever call her his?
Did she smile tenderly in saying this,
"I, only I, can give to him the bliss

For which he longs; I can his life make fair,
By granting in this one his every prayer,
And love permits me now his soul to save,
Yielding it all the love that it can crave?"

Did she through summer twilight sit alone,
  Marking with those intensely peaceful eyes
  The sweet and gradual changing of the skies?
And, as the birds stopped singing one by one,
  And all the sounds of day in lapsing light
  Grew silent, as the fast approaching night
  Shadow'd the world in peace, before her sight
Did he rise visioned in her solitude?
Ah! surely at such peaceful hours he stood
Before her, and her spirit saw his face,
Bright with the peace of the approaching days!

Did she the coming time anticipate,
  And murmur, "Through the deep'ning twilight
      come,
  O thou who lovest me, nor be thou dumb:
Call me again thy life, thy love, thy fate;
  Pour out thy love before me, let me see
  The very passion of it filling thee;
  For so, ah, doubly blessèd it shall be,

To answer, as I then shall make reply,
Oh, heart ! that thought to live unloved and die.
If love can bring thee heaven, ah ! surely then
Thou art no more unblessèd among men ?'

Ah, very sweet for such a soul as hers
  It must have been to sit and think how soon
  His clouded morn should grow to glorious noon
For sure the crowning joy that love confers
  On such high natures is the sense supreme
  Of being solely able to redeem
  The heart beloved, fulfilling all its dream,
Making a sad life joyous, saying, " Stand
Henceforth within the boundaries of Love's land."
Ah, doubtless then she carried in her breast
The double blessing of two hearts at rest.

Unworthy of her love he was, I know ;
  He but a minstrel singing in the night,
  Sad things and strange, unfitted for the light,
Made more for sombre shadows than the glow
  Of perfect morn transfiguring the sky.
  And if she heard from out the shade his cry
  Of bitter singing, and, approaching nigh,
Said softly, " Can you sing no song to prove
The bliss as well as sorrow of great love ?"

And made his heart to know, and lips to say,
How love has power to save as well as slay—

Yea, if her act were such and such her speech,
Is it for me to shame, with words ill said,
The soul her soul from out the darkness led,
To set in open daylight, in the reach
Of winds and all sweet perfumes? Time shall prove
Whether or not he would have shamed her love.
Till then I pray you that we stand aloof;
For darkness hides her now, and she has done
With loving any underneath the sun:
And he, *he* waits 'mid shadows sad and strange,
Till grief to rest, and life to death shall change.

AT A WINDOW.

THIS is the window at which she read,
That day in June when the heat mists rose,
Veiling the light of the sun o'erhead,
The poem, my heart the loveliest knows.
And here I sat near her feet, and fed
My heart with th' exquisite present, and said,
" The future may give, it may take away,
But she, she is with me one whole June day."

She read, I listened, and oft there came
The roses' scent from the paths below ;
My lips inaudibly named her name,
And, so great did the passionate worship grow,
It seemed I must weep to quench the flame,
Kindling and thrilling the blood of my frame ;
When her voice in compassionate music folded
The thoughts my heart to its longings moulded.

And here, one twilight in summer, too,
I, who had dreamed of her all the day,
Hearing the exquisite voice come through
The music of Nature, striving to say

A part of my love in lays I knew
That her spirit should one day own for true,
Was suddenly rapturously made aware
That she I dreamed of was with me there.

She bade me tell her my rhymes, and so
  I told them over, her mood to please;
My heart was full, and my voice was low,
  I knew she would speak, when my voice should
    cease;
She spoke: one minute I seemed to know,
All my life might be, if her life could flow
As one with mine, till the end were attained,
All grief and joy done with, the great rest gained.

And here I sit by myself to-night,
  Utterly lonely, hopeless of heaven,
Hearing no voice, discerning no light.
  Was not my life and my life's love given
Into her keeping, my sole delight?
And now she is far out of reach, out of sight,
What deed shall I do, what word shall I say?
What song shall I sing, and what prayer shall I pray?

"Dream thou no dream, though thy sleep be long,"
  To her I will say, "sleep fast, and well,

I—I will turn from the great world's wrong,
  Henceforward, alone with my grief to dwell.
I will pray to Love, I will sing a song,
That love shall keep pure, and passion make strong,
And the song thus born of my love shall be,
The star of my lady's divinity."

A DREAM.

I DREAMT I sat one evening all alone,
In chambers haunted by old memories,
No hope of star, or memory of sun
Lightened the grayness of the autumn skies,
My heart was full of sorrow, great and keen,
For there my Love one year with me had been;
There first my soul confessed her for its queen,
There had we mixed our kisses and our sighs,
There first to me her inmost heart was shown.

The wind outside was sweeping from the trees
Their few remaining leaves, as in some hall,
Where men have late held great festivities,
One plucks the faded glories from the wall,
Because the giver of the feast lies dead,
And those for whom the festal board was spread
Stand with sad faces round his silent bed,
And all the lamps that lit the festival
Untended burn and in the daylight cease.

Then suddenly I heard a voice, and lo!
  That voice was like the wind's voice having speech,
It said to me, "Rise up, dost thou not know
  Thy lady waits outside, and doth beseech
For entrance; shall she cry and thou not hear?"
I looked, but saw no living creature near,
Only that voice kept whispering in my ear,
  "She calls to thee, to thee her hands outreach,
Lo, by thy name she calls thee even now!"

I made no answer, but flung open wide
  The door, and faced the light with eager eyes;
I called her name with all my strength, I cried
  On that beloved name, as one who tries
To make men hear when in vext sleep he seems
To fly from pale avenging forms, and deems
He sleeps, but cannot waken from his dreams;
  I looked, and saw above the sad gray skies,
And the gaunt poplars standing either side.

And this was all I saw, and all I heard
  Was sad protracted moaning of the wind,
And piteous crying of some twilight bird,
  That came a nest in leafless boughs to find.
"Oh, false, false voice," I said, and turned away,

And shut the door upon the dying day,
And in the evening, desolate and gray,
  Sat still as one whom sorrow maketh blind,
And in the silence with my heart conferred.

And as I sat, I heard that voice again,
  And "Lo!" it cried, "be not discomfited,
Knocks she so loud, and calls she so in vain?
  Go forth once more, and call, nor be afraid
Of any fresh disaster. Heavenly state
She leaves for thee, and at thy very gate,
Worn in the wind and twilight, doth she wait."
  "I have no hope, for all thy words," I said,
"And yet I could not, if I would, refrain."

Then, as a man who, being near to die,
  Knowing men cannot save him, turns his face,
And calls on God, in his extremity,
  To lengthen yet a little while his days,
And, calling, feels withal he calls in vain,
So by her name I called her once again,
Then listened, and I heard the rush of rain,
  And sweep of winds down leaf-strewn garden ways;
I saw the blown clouds hurrying through the sky.

I looked, and listened, but no answer came,
  No form or phantom stood beside the door,
Only the wind, in moaning, moaned her name,
  Only my footsteps echoed on the floor;
And now the daylight died and darkness fell,
I did not know I dreamed, and yet the spell
Of dreaming seemed upon me; who shall tell
  If dreams are only dreams, or something more?
Who lights the depths of sleep with any flame?

And now that voice was silent; so I thought
  It is no voice at all that I have heard;
And now the wind and rain together wrought
  Wild sounds, and sweet, wherewith the night was stirred.
The hours bore on their dark and destined course;
Glad hearts and sad hearts slumbered, and the source
Of joy flowed on unnoticed, and the force
  Of grief was felt not; but my heart recurred
To that strange voice, whose tones the wind had caught.

Then, as I sat and pondered, suddenly
  In exultation woke again that voice;
It cried, "Rise up, go forth, for verily
  Thy love, she waits to clasp thee! hope decoys,

And men grow sick of hope, but this is truth ;
Thy kiss shall warm anew her cold sweet mouth ;
She left thee, but she kept with thee her troth,
  And now she comes from very far to thee,
And brings thee back with increase all thy joys."

Stung by these words, I could but count as vain,
  I flung the door back as in last disproof,
And there withal rushed in the wind and rain
  And there I saw the bleak night's starless roof,
And there and then I heard a voice divine,
And there two cold sweet hands took hold of mine,
And there a stormy star shone out for sign ;
  But all things were accomplished. "Oh, my Love,
Meet we so even in my dreams again !"

I brought her in, and hardly could believe
  For joy what was ; I know I could not speak,
I know I wept, yet not as those who grieve,
  I know her breath and lips were on my cheek,
I know I could not for a little space
Lift up my eyes and look upon her face ;
I know at last we met in wild embrace,
  I know I felt her lips to my lips cleave,
And how I felt by joy's excess made weak ;

And how my hands were fain her hair to stroke,
  Soft hair and bright, and how she bowed, and said—
And these, I think, were the first words she spoke—
  "Oh, Love, lay back upon my breast thy head,
Great love alone is changeless amid change;
Love hath the entire universe to range,
And hearts that love even death cannot estrange."
  At that word,—death, afresh the old wounds bled;
I turned to clasp her once again, and woke.

And long I pondered on the dream gone by,
  As men will ponder on an ancient scroll
That holds the key to some great mystery,
  Whose hidden meaning they would fain unroll.
Then said a voice unto me, without sound,
"So may the hope, long sought and never found,
Come when the last great darkness closes round—
  Come, and be apprehended by thy soul,
That thou mayst say, 'So meet we, she and I.'"

TO CICELY NARNEY MARSTON.

A BROTHER'S TRIBUTE.

WHAT were I, dear, without thee? Let me look
  Back on my earliest days, to-night, as he
Who, having thoroughly read through some book,
  Re-reads the opening pages lovingly.
In days when we were children, who but I
  Should know how thy soul turned from tender things,
How thy girl's heart would girlish joys put by,
  To share the boy's uncouth imaginings?

If then those days were sweet, who more than thou
  Made them so fair, blending thy life with mine?
What books we read together, then, as now!—
  Books that boys love, full of sea-winds and brine;
Do you remember that pet place of ours
  We called our haunt? Not beautiful it was,
Not musical with birds, nor gay with flowers,
  But from it we could watch the mad trains pass,

Whirling to places that we knew not of.
  Some vision in its smoke we must have seen ;
Heard music in its voice, now shrill, now rough,
  Or, there, our wanderings not so oft had been.
Oh ! days wherein all songs of birds were sweet,—
  The birds that mock us now with boisterous mirth ;
Days when we laughed for joy of summer-heat,
  Nor laughed less well when snow made white the earth !

Ah ! precious days we knew not how to prize !
  If they were slighted then, 'tis now their turn
To slight, and look from sad, reproachful eyes ;
  To whisper with white lips,—" In vain you yearn ;
You longed for other days, and they are come ;
  Now, you look back ; so, Dives, deep in Hell,
In torture looked at Lazarus, where, at home,
  He lay in Abraham's broad bosom.—Well,

" A gulf as deep is set 'twixt us and you,
  We cannot give you back the dream, the peace."
Alas ! we know their cruel words are true ;
  We never can re-capture one of these.
Did we not share our sorrows and our joys
  In later years, when we awoke, to find

Passion and sorrow in the deep sea's voice,
  A mighty mystery saddening all the wind?

Have we not loved the sea together, dear?
  Not as they love who come one hour a day,
To breathe its life, and then come not too near,
  Lest the waves take them in the face with spray;
But, when the July sun through waste blue skies,
  Declared the summer in her majesty;
When no sweet air, like a divine surprise,
  Came up from the scarce-stirring, breathing sea,

Yea, when the heat a fiery scourge became,
  And myriad shafts of sunlight charged the main,
In all that soundless violence of flame
  That made the shore one charr'd and smoking plain,
We did not fail at all! our eyes could pierce
  Between the blinding air and steaming beach,
To where, weighed on by summer, fair and fierce,
  The sea lay tranced in bliss too deep for speech.

Oh, silent glory of the summer day!
  How, then, we watched with glad and indolent eyes
The white-sailed ships dream on their shining way,
  Till, fading, they were mingled with the skies.

Have we not watched her, too, on nights that steep
  The soul in peace of moonlight, softly move
As a most passionate maiden, who in sleep
  Laughs low, and tosses in a dream of love?

And when the heat broke up, and in its place,
  Came the strong, shouting days and nights, that run,
All white with stars, across the labouring ways
  Of billows warm with storm, instead of sun,
In gray and desolate twilights, when no feet
  Save ours might dare the shore, did we not come
Through winds that all in vain against us beat
  Until we had the warm sweet-smelling foam

Full in our faces, and the frantic wind
  Shrieked round us, and our cheeks grew numb, then
      warm,
Until we felt our souls, no more confined,
  Mix with the waves, and strain against the storm?
Oh! the immense, illimitable delight
  It is, to stand by some tempestuous bay,
What time the great sea waxes warm and white,
  And beats and blinds the following wind with spray!

Have we not loved our France together? yea,
  More than our northern mother, be it said,

For there, oh, fuller is the life of Day,
  And all the earth seems sweeter to our tread :
We always grieved to leave her, always laughed
  For mere delight to see her face once more,
Tasting as wine the stainless airs that waft
  The sea-scents to the odours of the shore.

And we together have seen Italy,
  In kingly Genoa our steps have strayed,
And wandered by the famed and tideless sea ;
  Through Florence, in all loveliness arrayed,
Pure as a virgin, regal as a queen,
  Made great by many memories—a place
To see and die, contented having seen !
  Have we not worshipped her? Oh, nights and days !

Unlike our English nights and days, for there
  Each day's a sumptuous summer, and each night
A large and passionate caress of air,
  And Heaven grows one with Florence in God's sight !
And Venice we shall not forget, I deem ;
  Ah me ! the night we gained her, and you said,
"Weird as a city vision'd in a dream !"
  The winding watery streets before us spread ;

On either side we saw the houses stand
  Mystic and dark ! Of them I yearned to sing :
You said, " They seem built by no mortal hand,
  Yet wear a look of human suffering ! "
And then I knew my song might not avail
  More than those words to compass ; and that we,
When most remember'd things with Time turn pale,
  Should catch those houses rising from the sea !

Oh, in what things have we not been as one ?
  Oh, more than any sister ever was
To any brother ! Ere my days be done,
  And this my little strength of singing pass,
I would these failing lines of mine might show
  All thou hast been, as well as all thou art.
And yet what need ? for all who meet thee, know
  Thy queenliness of intellect and heart.

Oh, dear companion in the land of thought,
  How often hast thou led me by thy voice,
Through paths where men not all in vain have sought
  For consolation, when their cherished joys
Lie dead before them, never more to rise,
  And sing their souls to sleep, or in some place,
Busy with all life's work, with sudden eyes
  To flash upon them, till a rapturous space

Their souls yearn up, and lo! the lover sees
  His lady's face, where folded in love's calm
She waits at sunset 'neath her garden trees,
  Till they stand mouth to mouth, and palm to palm.
Now ebbs my song from thee, but as a waif
  The tide, receding, leaves upon the beach,
So, even this, my song's retreating wave,
  Leaves my soul nearer thine. Oh! poor vain speech

That fails so sadly when the heart o'erflows!
  Yet love me, dear, a little, for love's sake.
Shine thou upon my spirit till it grows
  Not all unlovely. If my life could take
Colour from thy life, I might learn to live,
  With no joy come to fruit; perceiving this,
It is not what we take, but what we give,
  That brings the peace more durable than bliss.

Bear with me, dear, a little longer yet;
  Forsake me not, if I forsaken stand.
Remember me! when others shall forget;
  Thy love to me is as thy precious hand
Might be upon my forehead if it burned
  In Hell, of some last fever; hold me fast,
Oh thou to whom in joy's full noon I turned
  As now I turn, the glory being past.

Sonnets from "Song-Tide."

SONNETS FROM "SONG-TIDE."

DESOLATE.

I STRAIN my worn-out sight across the sea,
I hear the wan waves sobbing on the strand,
My eyes grow weary of the sea and land,
Of the wide deep and the forsaken lea :
Ah ! love, return ! ah ! love, come back to me !—
As well these ebbing waves I might command,
To turn and kiss the moist deserted sand !
The joy that was, is not, and cannot be.
The salt shore, furrowed by the foam, smells sweet,
Oh ! blest for me, if it were now my lot,
To make this shore my rest, and hear all strife
Die out like yon tide's faint receding beat :
If he forgot so easily in life,
I may in death forget that he forgot.

WEDDED GRIEF.

AND now we walk together, she and I;
  She sits with me unseen where men are gay,
  And all the pleasures of the sense have sway;
She walks with me beneath the moonlit sky
And murmurs ever of the days gone by;
  She follows still in dreams upon my way,
  She sits beside me in the fading day,
And thrills the twilight silence with a sigh;
So on we journey till we gain the strand
Whose sea conjectures of no further land;
  There, where the past is fading from my view,
To this my sorrow I will reach my hand
And say—O thou who wert alone found true,
Forgive if now I must forget thee too.

A VAIN WISH.

I WOULD not, could I, make thy life as mine,
  Only I would, if such a thing might be,
  You should not, love, forget me utterly;
Yea, when the sultry stars of summer shine
On dreaming woods, where nightingales repine,
  I would that at such times should come to thee
  Some thought, not quite unmixed with pain, of me,
Some little sorrow for a soul's decline.
Yea, too, I would that through thy brightest times,
  Like the sweet burden of remembered rhymes,
That gentle sadness should be with thee, dear;
  And when the gates of sleep are on thee shut,
I would not even then, it should be mute,
But murmur, shell-like, at thy spirit's ear.

KNOWN TOO WELL.

Lo! now, how well I know the thing thou art;
Not more the colour of your hair and eyes
I know than all your various tones and sighs;
The laugh half-song, half-moan, that comes to part
The low clear voice, and placid as the heart,
Which, being stainless, needeth no disguise,
Serene and pure as moonlit seas and skies
Wherethrough no thunders roll, no lightnings dart.
The music of your voice by heart I have;
Yea, every tone, and semi-tone, I know;
The sound of taken breath, divinely sweet,
The touch of fingers, and the fall of feet;
I know you better than the wind the wave,
The sun the heavens, or the Alps the snow.

A DAY'S SECRET.

About the wild beginning of the Spring,
There came to me, and all the world, a day
To prove the Winter wholly gone away.
I said—'O Day, thy lips are sweet to sing,
But surely in thy voice some sweeter thing
Than thy mere song I find : lo, now I pray,
Before thou goest, turn to me and say,
Why round thee so my heart keeps wandering?'
Then, as a man who having loved and lost,
Within his dead love's sister's child may see
Something of what on earth he treasured most ;
So, looking on that day, my memory
Was filled with thoughts of April days wherein
Love's joy, too young for pain, did first begin.

PERSISTENT MUSIC.

Lo! what am I, my heart, that I should dare
 To love her, who will never love again:
 I, standing out here in the wind and rain,
With feet unsandalled, and uncovered hair,
Singing sad words to a still sadder air,
 Who know not even if my song's refrain—
 'Of sorrow, sorrow! loved, oh, loved in vain!'—
May reach her where she sits and hath no care.
But I will sing in every man's despite;
 Yea, too, and love, and sing of love until
My music mixes with her dreams at night;
 That when Death says to me, 'Lie down, be still!'
She, pausing for my voice, and list'ning long,
May know its silence sadder than its song.

THE WIND'S MESSAGE.

I SAID : 'What wouldst thou with my soul to-night,
Oh! wild March wind that wailest round the land?
Tell'st thou of some new grief even now at hand?
Or dost thou in thy swift and sounding flight
But chant a requiem for a past delight?
Like moan of billows on a distant strand,
Thy message which I fain would understand,
Comes down to me from Heaven's starless height.'
Then sadder wailed the wind, and sadder yet,
And swept with a great sudden rush of dole
Across me, till I cried, 'My lady's soul
Is stirred by Pity, and its currents set
To me-ward, and to me she bids thee say—
"Those prayed in vain, grieve more than those who pray."'

BRIEF REST.

O Love ! O lord of all delight, and woe !
For all who hear, thy voice is still the same ;
Thy hands cast down the body of wretched shame :
Still to thy chosen children thou dost show
The marvellous, sacred images that glow
Within thy inmost shrine where one deep flame,
Intense and clear, of colour without name,
Lights still the carven altars where they bow.
Brief rest is all I ask, O Love, of thee ;
A space wherein to look contentedly
Upon the beauty of my lady's face,
And mouth whereof the voice is its best praise ;
To feel the joy, and not the bitterness,
Of all her deep and silent loveliness.

DIVINE PITY.

I WONDER when you've gained the happy place,
  And walked above the marvel of the skies,
  And seen the brows of God, and large sweet eyes
Of Christ look lovingly upon your face,
  And all dear friends of unforgotten days;
Will you some time in that fair Paradise,
While all its peace and light around you lies,
  To greet your lover lost your dear eyes raise?
And when at length this thing you come to know,
  How he, forbid to pass, the heavenly bourne,
  Through undreamed distance roves with shades forlorn,
Will you be sorry, and, with eyes bent low,
  Wander apart the sudden wound to hide,
  And, meeting Mary, turn your face aside?

RETROSPECT.

OH! strange to me, and terrible it seems
To think that, ere I met you, you and I
Lived both beneath the same all-covering sky,
Had the same childhood's hopes and childhood's schemes,
And, later on, our beautiful false dreams:
The funerals of my dead joys passed me by,
And things, expected long, at length drew nigh.
The joy that slays and sorrow that redeems
Were ours before that day whereon we met;
And all the weary way that God had set
Between us was past over, and my soul
Knew in your fatal loveliness its goal.
'Twas mine to love, 'twas yours, sweet, to forget;
For you the haven, and for me the shoal.

BODY AND SOUL.

All know the beauty of my lady's face,
The peace and passion of her deep grey eyes,
Her hair wherein gold warmth of sunlight lies,
Her mouth that makes as mockery all praise,
And languorous low voice that hath such ways
Of unimagined music that the soul
Stands poised and trembling; breathless till the whole
Ends in an unhoped symphony of sighs:
But who as I my lady's soul shall know—
The deep tides of her nature that bear on,
Till all the line of common life seems gone,
To hearts that weary of their boundaries grow,
Then must I turn, O love, from thee to go
Through ways, to places, of thy soul unknown?

DISTANT LIGHT.

Oh, when, love, do I think upon thee most?
  When life looks blackest, and when hope seems dead,
  When darkness over all the past is shed,
When, as men hear upon some darkened coast
The distant tumult of the ocean's host,
  I hear the future sound in places dread
  Through which full soon my spirit must be led.
Then does my soul, through sorrow well-nigh lost,
  Look up to thy soul shining from afar,
  As men at sea look up to some fair star
Whose saving light may point the path to home.
  O love! bear with me for a little space,
  Bear with the roar and tumult of my days,
Till I am past the reach of wind and foam.

WHAT DO I LOVE?

WHAT is the thing for which I love thee best?
It taxes me to say; but this I know,
Thy tender regal beauty moves me so
That my heart beats and leaps within my breast,
As might the sea 'twixt narrow shores compressed.
Haply for this, or smiles that come and go
About thy mouth, or music sweet and low
Of thy clear voice, wherein is perfect rest,
Or for high intellect, that as a light
Lights up thy heart that straight illumes thy face,
Or for thy soul's deep tenderness that flows
Through every tone, and lingers in thy gaze—
For these known things I love with all my might,
And for the things beyond which no man knows.

BEFORE MEETING.

So we shall meet within a little space,
  And on the face wherein no love has birth
  Where nought is clear save beauty and the dearth
Of passions good or ill, I long shall gaze.
We shall not speak at all of vanished days,
  Of years that might have been, and made the earth
  All fair to me ; but words of little worth
Shall pass between us standing face to face.
  Too well I know the voice that I shall hear,
  When her lips, parting, let out sound more sweet
Than ever fell before on mortal ear.
  Oh, heart of mine, be strong until we meet,
Fill well thy *rôle* before her, O my heart,
Till death shall end the playing of thy part.

LOVE'S SELFISHNESS.

AND have I no more share in thee, O sweet,
  Than any of the many men who gaze
  Well pleased upon the beauty of the face,
Whose eyes are glad, indeed, your eyes to meet?
I, who have laid my soul beneath your feet,
  I, who upon the ruin of my days
  To thee an everlasting shrine will raise,
That men in coming years with song shall greet;
  I, even I, whose pride it is to bear
  The cross which thou hast laid upon me, love,
  Who give thee bitter songs, as men give prayer
To high and unknown gods, whom no prayers move;
I, who must long for thee through my life's night,
More than the blind man ever longed for light.

LOVE'S MAGNETISM.

O LOVE! though far apart our bodies be,
  I think my soul must somehow touch your heart,
  And make you, in the dusk of slumber start,
To feel my strong love beat and surge round thee,
Oh, one sweet island of my soul's waste sea.
  Serene, and fair, and passionless thou art,
  Why should my sorrow of thy life make part,
Or shade the face burnt in my memory?
I think, too, as I pace the tawny sand,
If you were on the opposite fair strand,
And my heart should with love to your heart yearn,
I do believe you would not choose but turn
And look across the sea, my way, until
Not knowing why, my soul should burn and thrill.

SONNETS TO A VOICE.

I.

Rossini, and Beethoven, and Mozart,
  And all the other men of mighty name
  Together joined their previous work to shame;
The subtlest mystery of their god-like art
To that most magic voice they did impart.
  Oh, from what kingdom of rare music came
  A voice on which alone might rest such fame
As never yet made glad one mortal's heart?
  A star of sound set far above the din
    And dust of life, a shade wherein to lie
Faint with the sudden ecstasy of bliss,
  A voice to drown remembrances of sin,
    A voice to hear and for the hearing die
As Antony for Cleopatra's kiss!

II.

A CLEAR voice made to comfort and incite,
Lovely and peaceful as a moonlit deep,
A voice to make the eyes of strong men weep
With sudden overflow of great delight;
A voice to dream of in the calm of night,
A voice—the song of fields that no men reap,
A treasure wrung by God himself from sleep!
A voice no song may follow in its flight,
A queenly rose of sound with tune for scent,
A pause of shadow in a day of heat,
A voice to make God weak as any man,
And at its pleadings take away the ban
'Neath which so long our spirits have been bent,
A voice to make death tender and life sweet!

III.

THERE is no sound at all in heaven now;
God and His angels bow from their high place
To hear the smallest word which that voice says,
And they do well indeed to listen so;
For they can hear it though its tones are low,
They must have learnt by heart its gracious ways,
Its fluctuant languor, and low laughter's grace—
Such tune as man again shall never know.
O winds! O birds! O rushing streams and seas!
And all things that make music for a space,
Dry up, grow mute; for one who hears that voice
Can no more in your lesser sounds rejoice.
O voice of rest, O amplitude of peace,
Sound deified—a bliss that beggars praise!

A VISION OF DAYS.

THE days whereof my heart is still so fain
  Passed by my soul in strange and sad procession,
  And one said—Lo, I held thy love's confession ;
And one—my hands were filled with golden gain
Of thy love's sweetnesses now turned to pain ;
  And one—I heard thy soul's last sad concession ;
  And one—for thee my voice made intercession ;
And one—I wept above thy sweet hopes slain.
Then followed, in a long and mournful band,
  Days wreathed with cloud and garmented with grey,
  And all made moan upon their weary way ;
But one day walked apart ; and, in her hand,
Before her face, she held a sorcerer's wand—
  And what she said I heard, but may not say.

PARTING WORDS.

GOOD-BYE, O love, once more I hold your hand :
  Good-bye, for now the wind blows loud and long ;
  The ship is ready, and the waves are strong
To bear me far away from this thy strand :
I know the sea that I shall cross, and land
  Whereto I journey, and the forms that throng
  Its palaces and shrines ; I know the song
That they alone can sing and understand.
  But promise me, O love, before I go
  That sometimes, when the sun and wind are low,
You, walking in the old familiar ways
Thronged with grey phantoms of the buried days,
  Will, looking seaward, say I wonder now
  How fares it with him in the distant place ?

PRESENTIMENT.

WHEN, after parting long and sore, we twain
  Met and stood soul to soul as face to face,
  While yet her hand in mine was, and her gaze
Made the blood burn and leap through every vein—
When thus, 'twixt risen joy and fallen pain,
  We stood with love in his own time and place,
  My soul had foresight of the coming days
When, parted, we should never meet again.
  O days expected long, and are ye here?
  Come ye with clouded brows and eyes austere,
Or with blithe faces making glad the sight,
  I know your song for curse, your laugh for jeer:
Which, then, is worse—your mockery of light,
Or the dumb darkness of the hopeless night?

LOVE'S MUSIC.

LOVE held a harp between his hands, and lo !
  The master hand, upon the harp-strings laid,
  By way of prelude, such a sweet tune played
As made the heart with happy tears o'erflow ;
But sad and wilder did that music grow,
  And, like the wail of woods by storm gusts swayed,
  While yet the awful thunder's wrath is stayed,
And Earth lies faint beneath the coming blow,
  Still wilder waxed that tune ; until at length
The strong strings, strained by sudden stress and sharp,
Of that musician's hand intolerable,
  And jarred by sweep of unrelenting strength,
  Sundered, and all the broken music fell.
Such was Love's music,—lo, the shattered harp !

NOT LIVED IN VAIN.

HAVE I not worshipped thee in tender lays,
And told in barren rhymes my love for thee;
And now I wish that I no more might see,
Or ne'er had seen your fair, alluring face;
Or, as a tune, felt your lithe body's grace
Melt through my heart that leap'd up eagerly
With joy of hope; now hope no more may be;
For hope lies dead, amid the dear, dead days.
Still, if the bitterness of unshed tears,
And burden of a spirit sorely tried,
Did e'er with joy of maiden's victory fill
Thy woman's heart, then surely these sad years
Have been well lived, nor, sweet, would I have died,
Till thy heart had of mine its perfect will.

SPEECHLESS.

Upon the Marriage of two Deaf and Dumb Persons.

THEIR lips upon each other's lips are laid ;
Strong moans of joy, wild laughter, and short cries
Seem uttered in the passion of their eyes.
He sees her body fair and fallen head,
And she the face whereon her soul is fed ;
And by the way her white breasts sink and rise,
He knows she must be shaken by sweet sighs ;
But all delight of sound for them is dead.
They dance a strange, weird measure, who know not
The tune to which their dancing feet are led ;
Their breath in kissing is made doubly hot
With flame of pent-up speech ; strange light is shed
About their spirits, as they mix and meet
In passion-lighted silence, 'tranced and sweet.

TO SLEEP.

O TENDER Sleep! Queen over ev'ry queen,
Our mother, since from thy deep womb we spring,
And unto thee return, and to thee bring
Our weary limbs and wearier hearts, and lean
Upon thy breast; thou who hast saddening seen
Our woe on earth, and blunted life's sharp sting,
And when we were in trouble did so sing,
That we forgot what was and what had been;
Open thy gentle arms and take me in;
Hide me! oh, hide me in thy mother's breast,
Between thy bosom sweet, and long, soft hair;
Yea, let me from thee drink the milk of rest:
Lay all my virtue level with my sin,
So that I have no thought of days that were.

SLEEPLAND GLORIFIED.

ALL nights my lady comes to me to rest,
Contentedly in quiet vales of sleep;
And sometimes, those sweet eyes of hers will weep,
And barren tears make wet each white, round breast.
Once only were her lips to my lips prest;
Then in my veins I felt love's passion leap,
And all the blood-red waves of pleasure sweep
Across my heart that might not be repress'd,
But found its vent in kisses thick and sweet,
That fell upon her mouth and quivering eyes,
While all her gracious body shook with sighs;
And we were wedded then, as was most meet.
No light shone round, no music breathed, save this:
Love's moan of joy, and murmur of his kiss.

SLEEPLAND FORSAKEN.

O LOVE ! O sweet ! where art thou gone, my love ?
I tread the songless ways of sleep alone ;
In sleepland's shadowy caves I make my moan.
O sleep's pale, waveless, voiceless seas whereof
She seemed a part—where is the siren gone ?
O whispering forests, tell me of the dove !
O paths with lilies and with roses sown,
Where is my flower, the fairest of the grove ?
O sweet unanswering voice and feet so flown,
In vain along the silent shore I rove
Where shadows of the moon-lit rocks lie prone,
By tideless seas that never winds may move !
Alas, my God, their depths are deep enough
To hide that face, and they shall keep their own.

THE FIRST KISS.

SHE sat where he had left her all alone,
With head bent back, and eyes through love on flame,
And neck half flushed with most delicious shame,
With hair disordered, and with loosened zone;
She sat, and to herself made tender moan,
As yet again in thought her lover came,
And caught her by her hands and called her name,
And sealed her body as her soul his own.
The June moon-stricken twilight, warm, and fair,
Closed round her where she sat 'neath voiceless trees,
Full of the wonder of triumphant prayer,
And sense of unimagined ecstasies
Which must be hers, she knows, yet knows not why;
But feels thereof his kiss the prophecy.

CONJECTURE.

I THINK, love, as I hold your hand in mine,
If starless, cheerless, everlasting night
Should settle suddenly upon my sight,
And I should no more see your eyes divine,
Or golden lights that in your tresses shine,
Or face now made my measureless delight,
Or sweet curved throat, warm, beautiful, and white,
Or soft, lithe arms that round about me twine,
How should I bear to sit with you as now,
And if you looked upon me not to know;
To hear men praise your throat, mouth, eyes, and hair,
Yet feel to me you were no longer fair?
To miss the blush that colours all your kiss,—
Slay me outright, O God! but spare me this.

Sonnets from "All in All."

SONNETS FROM "ALL IN ALL."

NOT THOU BUT I.

It must have been for one of us, my own,
  To drink this cup and eat this bitter bread.
  Had not my tears upon thy face been shed,
Thy tears had dropped on mine ; if I alone
Did not walk now, thy spirit would have known
  My loneliness, and did my feet not tread
  This weary path and steep, thy feet had bled
For mine, and thy mouth had for mine made moan ;
  And so it comforts me, yea, not in vain,
To think of thy eternity of sleep,
To know thine eyes are tearless though mine weep :
  And when this cup's last bitterness I drain,
One thought shall still its primal sweetness keep—
Thou hadst the peace and I the undying pain.

POSSIBLE MEETING.

ART thou afar or near, oh Royal Day—
  Thou Day that bring'st me to my love again?
  Must the sweet autumn moon be in the wane,
Before I feel thy breath, and hear thee say,
"Behold thy love?" or shall the skies be gray,
  Disturb'd by wind and sense of imminent rain,
  Before I hear thee cry, "Oh, not in vain
Thou didst beseech my coming in thy lay?"
  Or shall the leaden winter be begun,
  And all the sky forsaken of the sun?
  Let this be as it may, my thoughts outrun
The dull and hostile days that intervene;
They shall not bar thee, conqueror and queen,
But be thy guards when thou dost crown'd pass in.

LOVE'S ANSWER.

I SAID to Love, " Lo, one thing troubles me !
  How shall I show the way in which I love ?
  Is any word, or look, or kiss enough
To show to her my love's extremity ?
What is there I can say, or do, that she
  May know the strength and utter depth thereof ?
For words are weak, such love as mine to prove,
  Though I should pour them forth unceasingly."
Then fell Love's smile upon me, as he said,
  "Thou art a child in love, not knowing this ;
  That could she know thy love by word or kiss,
Or gauge it by its show, 'twere all but dead :
  For not by bounds, but shoreless distances,
Full knowledge of the sea is compassèd."

PRELUDES.

I.

As looking on a river that progresses
  Through some loud, populous city, till it gains
  The acrid sea—thought tracks it through the plains
O'er which it flowed, to innermost recesses
Of hills the earliest light of morn caresses,
  Where, nursed by Nature, fed by fragrant rains,
  Sung to by birds, swayed by all varying strains
Of winds the very soul of spring possesses,
  It sprang a slender stream, which, gath'ring force,
Grew to a river hurrying to the sea;
So, on this current of my song look ye.
  Think not upon its dark unalterable course,
Nor of drowned hopes that in its eddies be;
But dream ye know and wander near its source.

II.

NOT as who gives to some belovèd one,
  Some dear belovèd one whose altered eyes
  May not the face above them recognise,
The roses he has taken from the sun
To deck her cold sweet body, saying, "None
  Shall give thee gifts hereafter,"—one rose lies
  Upon the breast that doth not sink or rise,
And in the hand whose pressures are all done
  Another rests,—not so to thee, my love,
Give I these songs of thee ; I do but give
Because I love and for thy memory live ;
  As swaying pines, that winds to dirges move,
Give to the winds again what the winds have given,
Give I these songs to thee, my life and my heaven."

III.

Go down, my songs, now to the land unknown,
  The starless kingdom that has Death for king.
  About the silent porches close and cling.
Through breezeless air, where bird hath never flown,
Or waste, gray fields, wherein no flower hath blown,
  Hills from whose barren bosom wells no spring,
  Let your tones rise, and die in echoing;
And by their sadness let my love be shown.
  Then, like the echo lasting, it may be
A voice shall answer; but if otherwise,
  Cease not! nor strive to solve Death's mystery,
For she may hear you, though no voice replies.
  Go then! and say, "He follows in our wake,
  Who bade us hasten here for his love's sake."

NOT DEATH, BUT LIFE.

I AM not dead, beloved, would I were!
  My spirit has not ceased to beat with thine;
  Only my hope is dead; and peace divine
Lies dead upon Hope's tomb, while black Despair,
Repeating ever an unanswered prayer,
  Gives me to drink his sacramental wine,
  And sacramental bread to eat, in sign
That I am his till death, his robes to bear.
  I am not dead! I have not died with thee.
This is no sleep, perpetual as time.
  Dead lips are mute, and dead eyes cannot see
Pale memories and half-dreamed dreams of bliss;
  Dead feet have rest, but living feet must climb
The steep, round which the eternal darkness is.

LIFELESS LIFE.

SINCE we, for the last time, "good-bye" have said,
  Since I may never hold thy hands again,
  And prayers are useless, and all tears are vain,
What do I hear, when round thy soul are spread
Silence and sleep, and on my spirit shed
  The bitter, uncompassionating pain,
  Till my heart yearns for rest, as earth for rain
When by the utter sun discomfited?
  So, a blind man within some storied hall
May hear men round him press, and one voice praise
The deep enchantment of a pictured face,
  One this sheer stretch of sea, and one the fall
Of April sunlight on some green wet place,
  While *he* stands sightless between wall and wall.

FOREDOOMED.

No star upon thy course sheds any ray;
  Though thy bark bear for years the wind and foam,
  To no sweet haven shall it ever come.
The night shall see thee drifting, and the day
Behold thee as the night; thou shalt not pray,
  Nor utter any cry, but, cold and dumb,
  Watch the waves pass, and glad ships sailing home
Shall hail thee not upon thy trackless way.
The salt wave shall taste bitter to thy lip:
  Weary, yea, unto death, thy soul shall be
  Of winds, and the interminable sea,
That does not bring thee nearer any goal,
But sweeps through changeless gloom the fated ship
To its remote, inevitable shoal.

TOO LATE.

LOVE has its morn, its noon, its eve, and night.
We never had the noontide, never knew
The deep, intense, illimitable blue
Of fervid, mid-day heavens, making bright
With princely liberality of light
Waters the water-lily trembles through ;
But, in the evening's shadow did we two
Set out to gain Love's farthest, fairest height.
O love ! too late, too late for this we met ;
The goal was near, the nightfall nearer yet.
One star of Memory lightens in our track,
And all the rest is dark ; I will go back—
Back to the paths we walked in, and there stay,
Until I change them for the silent way.

AN UNKNOWN TONGUE.

BECAUSE my life is dark and desolate,
  Like some gray, uninhabitable land,
  Which hears for ever on its wreck-strewn strand,
The roar of waves inimical as fate;
Because I cry life's bitterest cry too late;
  Because pale Grief, with her relentless hand,
  Leads me up paths most steep, until I stand
Alone before the shut and shadowy gate
  Which opens once to each, and only once,
Would I make your lives sad, all ye who say
"Bright are the skies above, and fair the way,
  Darkness may come, the present is the sun's!"
Love knows I would not; fear not then my song,
I speak strange words; ye know not yet the tongue.

THE DEAD HOPE.

THE mother who has lost her only child,
Thinking of all she should have been to her;
What time strange voices in the breezes stir,
Sits in the Autumn twilight, gray and wild,
Remembering how the dead lips spoke and smiled.
And as she sits, her child full grown and fair,
Large eyed, with glory of up-gathered hair,
Comes in a vision exquisitely mild.
So, sometimes, as in dreams, *I* seem to see
That joy arisen to full height, that life,
That hope which died in shining infancy.
The mother yet may be a fruitful wife
And bear fresh children; but for me there springs
No second hope from out the womb of things.

WEDDED MEMORIES.

AND if my memory live when I am dead,
  When all whereby men knew me turns to dust;
  When deaf, and dumb, and sightless, I am thrust
Into dank darkness, where the worms are fed
By Death's gaunt hand, that breed in my cold bed;
  When I, at last, with life and love break trust;
  When the soul's yearnings and the body's lust,
Are ended wholly as a tune out-played;
  If then, men name my name, and from these lays
The depth and glory of thy soul divine,
Shall not, beloved, my memory live in thine?
  Our memories moveless 'mid the moving days,
Intense and sad like changeless stars that shine
  On ruined towers of a predestined race.

SAD MEMORIES.

If two who love when I am gone from hence
  To some far distant land across the seas,
  Should in this room, possessed by memories,
Sit wrapt in love's calm, holy and intense,
Feeling their passionate kisses recompense
  Their hearts for doubts and fears now lost in peace
  That manifold embraces but increase,
Aware in all of Love's omnipotence—
  Would they not, sitting silent, feel the weight
Of some unknown despair upon them press?
  Would they not taste the sorrow of our fate?
Would not some black foreboding smite them there?
Would they not feel and hear the tireless stress
Of phantom wings through the love-bewildered air?

DEATHWARD WAYS.

ALL men and women walk by various ways
  To Death's dark land; and some with song and mirth
  Beguile the time which lies 'twixt death and birth;
Some, joyous and full blooded, through a maze
Of splendid passionate nights and dreamy days,
  Gain soon their goal; and some who find a dearth
  Of joy in all, poor strangers on the earth,
Plod on their path, and yield nor prayer nor praise.
  But, look you, I will walk with none of these,
I walk a straight and solitary path;
A way which no sweet scent or verdure hath,
  And as I walk, like strong and rising seas,
I hear my whole past surging on my track,
And would return, yet never may go back.

WAS IT FOR THIS?

WAS it for this we met three years ago;
Took hands, spake low, sat side by side, and heard
The sleeping trees beneath us touched and stirred
By some mild twilight wind as soft as snow,
And with the sun's late kisses still aglow?
Was it for this the end was so deferred?
For this thy lips at length let through the word
That saved my soul, as all Love's angels know?
Was it for this, that sweet word being said,
We kissed and clung together in our bliss,
And walked within Love's sunlight and Love's shade?
Was it for this—to dwell henceforth apart,
One housed with death, and one with beggared heart?
Nay, surely, love, it was for more than this.

SORE LONGING.

My body is athirst for thee, my love;
  My lips, that may not meet thy lips again,
  Are flowers that fail in drought for want of rain;
My heart, without thy voice, is like a grove
Wherein no bird makes music, while, above,
  The twilight deepens as the low winds wane;
  My eyes, that ache for sight of thee in vain,
Are hidden streams no stars make mirrors of.
  I see thee but in memory, alas!
So some worn seaman, restless in his sleep,
In time of danger, o'er the raging deep,
  Sees visionary lights, and cries, "We pass
The prayed-for land; reverse the helm, put back!"
And still the ship bears on her starless track.

DIVINE POSSIBILITY.

BECAUSE no man who lives can surely tell
  What thing comes after death, each night and day,
  Unheard of any but of Love, I say,
"O Love, my lord and master, from the spell
Of bitter sweetnesses that end in Hell,
  Keep thou my soul ; strange forms beset my way,
  And as I pass, they whisper to me, 'Stay!
And rest with us, and life shall yet be well.'
  So guide me, Love, that if, at end of all,
I should awake, and to my eyes be shown
  Her face in heaven, and her voice should call
My soul to her, that soul then free from stain,
Strengthen'd by love and purified by pain,
May answer. and reclaim her for its own."

VAIN DREAMS.

I AND my love are parted; many days,
  Sad days must be before we meet again;
  But surely we shall meet, and all the pain
Of separation die as we embrace,
When on her bosom lies again my face,
  And lips dissevered reunite and strain
  Together in a kiss that shall enchain
Our souls too much for any speech of praise.
  And when at length we speak I think I know
Of what our speech shall be. Oh, vain my soul!
  Put by these dreams, take up thy load and go;
Each lot, however bitter, hath its goal.
  Thy goal is death, not life, and when life ends
  The night that hides thy love, on thee descends.

DEAD!

"DEAD, my beloved, what means this word?" I say,
Over and over, as I fain would wring
Some hidden meaning from it; let me bring
My soul to comprehend it. Gone away!
Asleep, to wake no more on any day?
Nay, not asleep, awake, and wandering
Through lands of bloom in a continuous Spring!
I seek for light, yet find no certain ray;
But this I know, again we shall not meet;
We never more shall sit as we have done,
Breathless with love, in twilight hushed and sweet;
Upon no joy of ours shall set the sun;
Nor more nor less than this it means; and yet,
Can I remember so and thou forget?

IMPOSSIBLE JOY.

WHAT of that place, my dearest, the far place
  We should have seen together, planning so,
  Before the Autumn's winds had strength to blow,
And Summer turn'd from us with lingering gaze,
As one who, parting, yet to go delays ?—
  Ah ! very strange, it seems to me, to know
  That seasons in that place still come and go,
Though we come not ; if down the talked-of ways
  My solitary steps are ever led,
  I shall seem surely as some man new-wed,
Who finds the loved one absent from his side,
And seeing she returns not, opens wide
  The bridal chamber, and bows down his head
Upon the couch where should have lain the bride.

A PARABLE.

THERE was a man who bore for many days
  Pains, sore to bear, that would not let him rest ;
  Meanwhile, great fear of death upon him press'd,
Till, lo ! he dreamed and slept ; and full of grace
The dream was, for a strange and holy place
  Was open'd to him, and on God's own breast
  He lay, with all his sins and fears confess'd,
Having Christ's saving kiss upon his face :
  " And very sweet it is," he said, " to know
That life at length is over, and grief done."
  Then fell the dream away from him, and lo !
He woke, to find another day begun,
  Yea, woke to bear more agony and dread,—
  Death, hanging with gaunt face, above his bed.

THE DARK WAY.

WHEN first I knew this trouble of my days,
This unrelenting grief, I was like one
Who, suddenly made blind, walks not alone,
Nor yet for any other guidance prays,
But silent sits, conjecturing of the ways
That he must walk, the perils he must shun,
Unaided by the light of star or sun;
And as at length, with set and vacant gaze,
He rises, stumbles, stops, moves on again,
Trusting, withal, his feet a path have found,
Distinguishing the day from night, by sound;
So I, through tortuous paths no light makes plain,
Having less even than the blind man's faith,
With outspread hands, grope my dark way to Death.

GRIEF AGAINST GRIEF.

BETTER, my love, than this to love in vain,
To feel what time my heart was sad for love,
Thy soul unpitying stand from mine aloof;
Better to bear the torment and the pain
Of lips that from all worship must refrain,
So I might feel thy sweetness near me move;
Touch thee, and see thee, find some way to prove
That souls can love, themselves not loved again.
But thus to sit without thee, and to know,
No grief the past can ever recreate,
To seek, and not to find thee; to awake,
And face the haggard day that can bestow
No gift of love; these are such griefs as make
Man feel he is but man, while fate is fate.

COMPLETE SACRIFICE.

I DO not ask thee, Love, to make life sweet;
All thou hast lain upon me I must bear:
Nor do I once again for any share
In things I once held dear; but when I meet
With sore temptation, and my pulses beat
With bodily desire, and so despair
Half drags me from the path, and makes me fare
Like men whose lips her lips did never greet,—
In such an hour, stand close, and hear my call,
Lighten my darkness and sustain my feet:
Chain me in chains which, if they bruise, control;
That I may make this sacrifice complete,
Which is, indeed, no sacrifice at all,
Except I yield the body with the soul.

FATE.

GOD knows I had no hope before she came,
  And found me in the darkness, where alone
  I sat, even then, and brooded o'er things flown.
She touched my hand, she called me by my name,
She broke my darkness up, and smote with flame
  The heights and depths of life, till I was shown
  Where possible heavens lay, and things long known
As things transfigured in that light became.
  I sought my heaven, her love, at whose white gate,
"Oh! my beloved, take me in," I cried.
  A little while the answer was delayed;
  And then her voice, from out the glory, said:
"Enter! and be at peace;" and Fate replied:
  "Thy love is strong, but stronger is my hate!"

PROPHETIC MOMENTS.

As when one wandering in a wood by night,
  Hearing the owls cry down the dark for prey,
  Seeing no star to light him on his way,
In those dread moments feels the entire might
Of some great distant grief his whole soul smite
  With sickening apprehension of a day,
  The fruit of years unborn, till waste and gray
His far life looks in the soul's prophetic sight;
  So sometimes through the horror of my days,
The sights and sounds of ghostly memories,
  I stray; but the mysterious sadness through
My soul is reached by breaths of some high peace;
  Airs from a fair far land I never knew,
  A land wherein she walks with Love, and prays.

LOVE'S BIRTH-HOUR.

WHAT was the day when, sweet, I loved thee first?
  The day when my heart trembled at thy tone
  Almost as much as would my lips have done
Could they have slaked at thine their new-born thirst?
When did this passion into full flower burst,
  As a bud into a rose, beneath the sun?
  When felt I first, my body and soul as one?
Life with thee bless'd, without thee, empty, and curs'd?
  Who notes Love's birth-hour then? In sooth not I;
Though Love like all things hath its birth and growth,
  And love at first sight is a short-lived thing;
  Nor shall I know the hour when Love must die,
For that will be my death-hour too, and both
  Will pass to where is no remembering.

TREASURED THOUGHTS.

IF one you loved had tarried 'neath your roof,
And wrought with her sweet fingers many a change,
Would you, when she had left you, disarrange
Her handiwork, the veritable proof
Of her late presence? Nay, for very love
You would not; but in memory would range
Through rooms her presence had left sweet and strange,
And nought from where she placed it would remove;
So when she came into my life's dark ways,
Her soul gave many a saving thought to mine,
And all she gave of her abundant grace,
I treasure in my heart, as most divine!
That if we meet again, in far off days,
They may be found, as offerings on a shrine.

WASTED SPRING.

ONCE more, though late, comes back to us the spring !
  May's sunbeams waver in the wavering trees,
  And leaves and grasses sing in the singing breeze ;
The time hath come for nightingales to sing :
And, suddenly, one day in June may bring
  From fields wherein 'twere good to lie at ease,
  Life-giving, as the perfume of blown seas,
The warm, keen smell of hay, bewildering
  The sense with its sharp sweetness ; but to-day,
Notes solemn, and sad, and measured, have I heard—
  The cuckoo's desolate cry presaging ill,
  Telling of falling leaves, cold skies, and gray.
Make the Spring hopeless then, prophetic bird,
  Since that one voice eternally is still.

ARRESTED SPRING.

THE Spring has been here; thus much, ye can tell;
Behold these half-unfolded leaves that lie
Upon the path, beneath an ashen sky.
Within these boughs, transfixed as by a spell,
Songless the song-birds sit; there is a smell
Of Spring about, but that sweet smell shall die,
As streams the west wind freed sink stagnantly,
Because, last night, a blight on all things fell.
What will ye hope, then, in this desolate place?
Will ye intreat the Winter to make good
His promise; and with cold and lustrous grace,
Change to a chrysolite the tender bud?
Not so, all energy that change could bring
Lies mute; arrested, with the arrested Spring.

AUTUMN QUIET.

THE splendours of the summer time are done,
And, though the roses linger for a space,
Soon will they fade on paths and garden ways.
The russet leaves lie thickly and the sun
Wakes late now and his course is swiftly run.
No passionate summer storm the night dismays
With flame and thunder ; these veiled nights and days
We would not seek, yet, having, hardly shun.
Then said a voice, I knew for Love's—" Even so
May thy life be, dost thou my will and hers—
A passionless existence that shall flow
Like some tamed stream which men have wrought to go
For ever in one course, which no wind stirs
To speed or wreck the burden that it bears?"

PRAYER.

OH, Love, behold how steep the path has grown—
Almost too steep for any feet to tread ;
To thee I call, to thee I bow my head.
In solitude with men, but still alone,
My heart hath made perpetually its moan.
Yea, as the living call upon the dead,
Stretching their emptied arms across the bed
Where lies what yesterday they called their own,
So have I called on thee ; but what avails !
Sorrow, grown mad and impious, dominates,
And memory in the darkness sits and wails ;
At every step some foe in ambush waits
To snare my feet. Oh, Love, rise up, awake,
And save me swiftly for thy mercy's sake.

THE ONE GRACE.

I KNOW my strength of singing scant and brief,
  Nor can I hope that men my words shall heed
  When I, in death, of love have little need.
I have not taught you wisdom out of grief,
And in myself have I had no belief—
  Said few wise words and done no worthy deed,
  Too faint to follow, powerless to lead—
A helmless vessel dashed from reef to reef.
  But if, dear friends, you speak of me at all,
Say in my favour this, and this alone :
That when Love was in her made manifest,
  I knew her for my queen, and, leaving all,
Followed the noblest and the loveliest
Until I knelt before her at Love's throne.

LIFE AND DEATH.

How is it then with her? I think 'tis well;
  She hath no memory of days that were,
  Her soul is vexed by no importunate prayer.
Love bowed beside her when on sleep she fell,
No wanderer knocketh at her gates to tell
  Of things she would not know. She hath no care
  For any love. Our lives lie waste and bare
Like lands whose losses make them memorable,
And still she heedeth not; yea verily,
Oh, life and love, if such a thing could be,
  That we for one brief minute should forget,
  She would not sigh or smile to know. And yet,
While life is sad and death is even thus,
Can all be well with her and ill with us?

JUNE.

Oh, June, thou hast too many memories;
  Ghosts walk by daylight 'neath thy steadfast sun—
  And people thy warm darkness; can I shun
These faces of dead joys and pitiless eyes
That look in mine till my pierced spirit cries—
  "Forbear—pass by!" and makes its desolate moan
  For pity of its sorrow spent and prone?
Amid these ghosts my heart lies faint and dies:
Oh, summer twilight, sad beyond all telling,
  Oh, nights made once for love, made now for grief!
  Come, winter, with thy formidable array
Of frost and storms the gray cold ocean swelling!
  Yet wherefore come? Thou can'st bring no relief;
  Hast thou not too the memories that dismay?

WHAT PROFITS IT?

ALAS, my God! what profits it at all—
  The passionate love, the grief, the short-lived bliss,
  The pregnant silence after the long kiss,
The words half uttered and half heard, the fall
Of bitter tears, the long unanswered call
  Of heart to heart, the anguish and the fear;
  And then the life lived after, chill and drear
As one long winter day when no sun is;
The hourly strife with unseen enemies,
  The pitiable armistice, and then
The strife resumed; failures and victories;
  And yet no rest to either side till when
  Death, that is mightier than the loves of men,
Makes all at once an everlasting peace?

DESOLATE LOVE.

I SAW Love sitting by a dry well head,
  No crown was on his hair, and in his hand
  He had no sceptre but a warrior's brand;
With blood his hands and feet and robes were red,
And ever as he bowed his face he shed
  Most bitter tears, and cried, " Where is my land—
  And all my subjects that might not withstand
My perfect will and the sweet words I said?
  Lo! men have turned from me in these dark days,
The temples that I reared they have cast down."
  Then close by his shone out my lady's face,
I saw her bow, and knew she spoke with him,
And when he raised his eyes they were not dim,
And on his hair was glory of a crown.

QUANTUM MUTATUS!

WITH emptied outstretched hands and downcast eyes
  Love walks alone and walks uncomforted;
  And if the aureole gleam about his head
I hardly know; his lips are full of sighs,
And they who question him gain no replies.
  Only to me he saith, "My feet have bled
  From many a thorny path, and I have said
Such grievous words as make the swift tears rise.
  But never since men knew my awful name
Have I walked thus by such precipitous ways,
  Seen such deep darkness, and illusive flame
Which leaves no track. Oh, great ancestral days!
  For I am he whose mighty power and peace
  Crowned Helen—consecrated Beatrice."

DREAMING LOVE.

I SAW Love in a strange and hidden place;
  His face was as the face of one who dreams,
  Yea, as some weary slumberer's who seems,
By the glad smile which lightens all his face,
To walk once more 'mid old loved country ways,
  What time the tender April twilight teems
  With songs, and gusts of lilac, and the streams
Run with the sound of wind through some green maze.
  Love's hands were folded on his quiet breast.
But lo, a far-off voice called, "Love, arise;
  The night is ended and the dream is done."
Then Love unclosed his fair and mournful eyes,
  Took up his staff, and turned him from his rest,
  And as he went shone round his path the sun.

LOVE'S SUFFICIENCY.

If love is insufficient, what avails?
  If love abideth not, then what thing stays?
  One prayed to wearies as the one who prays,
The exquisite delight of passion fails,
No joy endures, the brightest beauty pales,
  And though to art we give our nights and days,
  We know our brows unworthy of their bays,
Wreckt men whose eyes see visionary sails.
  And is love insufficient, oh, my queen?
Did we not say, when in love's sweet control
  We stood, each bound to each—"For what hath been
This hour suffices?" Oh, belovèd, see
It hath sufficed. Love's saving memory
Has interposed 'twixt ruin and my soul.

LOVE AND DEATH.

"My gracious lady talks with Love," I said,
"Yet hath perchance no thought of me.—Oh, sweet,
See now I put my heart beneath your feet,
Having no crown to set upon your head.
Is the gift too unworthy?" Then Love led
My lady up to me and bade her greet
My lips with hers, that body and soul might meet.
We kissed, we clung together comforted.
"My lady talks with me," I said; "Love's grace
Hath made us now for ever more as one."
My lady turned aside, and lo! one saith,
"Lover, behold thy lady talks with Death."
I turned to clasp my sweet, but in her place
Death towered before me and eclipsed the sun.

SUMMER TWILIGHT.

SOME natures seem, like days in early spring,
  Soft and most changeful, fair with light and shade;
  And some are like gray autumn days that spread
A chill on all they meet; and others bring
A sense of patience and mute suffering,
  Like summer days whereon the heat has made
  Such sudden silence that the wind seems dead,
And the sun's light is veiled from everything;
But her deep nature I may liken to
  A bounteous summer twilight, when one knows
  An unimagined heaven of repose,
From which a new heaven opens to the view,
  While there unfolds within the heart the sense
  Of some divine unknown omnipotence.

THE UTTERED SOUL.

If God to me had given the heart and brain
  Of some musician skilled above the rest,
  Her soul in music had been manifest :
Perchance some painter, frenzied to sweet pain
By her deep loveliness, through stress and strain
  Of great desire to be through life possessed
  Of all that beauty, had been crowned and blessed,
And, spent yet living, seen the light strike plain
  Upon her deathless loveliness, and died !
But Music could alone her spirit render ;
  Long waves of passionate melody that roll
  Wave after wave all tending to one goal,
Pure notes, intense beyond all language tender,
  Her soul in music, Music deified !

LOVE'S QUEST.

Love walks with weary feet the upward way,
 Love without joy and led by suffering;
 Love's unkissed lips have now no song to sing,
Love's eyes are blind and cannot see the day,
Love walks in utter darkness, and I say:
 "Oh, Love, 'tis summer," or, "Behold the spring,"
 Or, "Love, 'tis autumn, and leaves withering,"
And "Now it is the winter bleak and gray,"
 And still Love heedeth not. "Oh, Love," I cry,
"Wilt thou not rest? the path is over steep:"
 Love answers not, but passeth all things by;
Nor will he stay, for those who laugh or weep.
 I follow Love who follows Grief; but lo,
Where the way ends, not Love himself can know.

Sonnets from "Wind-Voices."

SONNETS FROM "WIND-VOICES."

ALONE.

NOT as of old times do I come to-day
  To breathe the strength and freshness of the sea
  Until as part of it I seemed to be—
Part of the sea-wind and the blowing spray;
She who once came with me is far away,
  For Death was kind to her, though cruel to me,
  And all my empty life drifts aimlessly,
Like vessels that no more their helms obey.

Oh sea that had my childish love and hers,
  What message from my dead one dost thou bring?
Surely with me through thee her soul confers,
  In some inexplicable way to wring
  Mine eyes with bitterest tears, remembering
What no more lights my dark, disastrous years.

LOVE AND MUSIC.

I LISTENED to the music broad and deep—
  I heard the tenor in an ecstasy
  Touch the sweet, distant goal, I heard the cry
Of prayer and passion, and I heard the sweep
Of mighty wings, that in their waving keep
  The music that the spheres make endlessly;
  Then my cheeks shivered, tears made blind each eye
As flame to flame I felt the quick blood leap,
And, through the tides and moonlit winds of sound,
  To me love's passionate voice grew audible.
Again I felt your heart to my heart bound,
  Then silence on the viols and voices fell;
  But, like the still, small voice within a shell,
I heard Love thrilling through the void profound.

A DREAM.

Here—where last night she came, even she, for whom
I would so gladly live or lie down dead,
Came in the likeness of a dream and said
Some words that thrilled this desolate ghost-thronged room—
I sit alone now in the absolute gloom.
Ah! surely on her breast was leaned my head,
Ah! surely on my mouth her kiss was shed,
And all my life broke into scent and bloom.
Give thanks, heart, for thy rootless flower of bliss,
Nor think the gods severe though thus they seem,
Though thou hast much to bear and much to miss,
Whilst thou thy nights and days to be canst deem
One thing, and that thing veritably this—
The imperishable memory of a dream.

THE HEAVEN OF HEAVENS.

NOT to the general heaven take thy flight,
O happy, happy, happy song of mine;
But to the heart of the inmost heaven divine,
O'er fields of day to privacies of light,
Take thou thy way, and, being come aright
To that fair place which is my heaven and thine,
Where my thoughts throng, as pilgrims to a shrine,
Even to her heart, whose love is my soul's sight;
Say unto her that other songs are free
To sound about the world and win men praise;
Thy greater glory is this sovereign grace
To live alone in her sweet memory—
To have thy heavenly and abiding place
In her deep heart, Love's holiest sanctuary.

HOPE.

I SAID, "Who art thou with the flower-crowned hair
And shining eyes?" She answered, "I am Hope,
Thy friend for life, with all thy foes to cope."
Sweet songs she sang me, of far lands and fair,
Her face made starlight in a starless air;
But once, as down a dark and flowerless slope
That heard the sea, we strove our way to grope,
A sudden terror came upon her there;

She fell—the strength ebbed from her, and she died.
Above her, dead, in body and soul I bowed,
While with strange tongues the darkness was endowed,
And well I knew the thing they prophesied.
Then up the shore came the waves large and loud,
And my life answered, tide to bitter tide.

IN EARLY SPRING.

WITH delicate wind, clear light of the warm sun,
  Surely I know how subtly sweet is Spring,
  The earth and man's worn heart revisiting.
I would not have thy brief existence done,
And yet I would, O new-born Spring, that one
  Might meet thine eyes without their mirroring
  The ghost of many a sweet and bitter thing—
Old dreams, old hopes, too frail to lean upon.
O last descended of a hostile race,
  Though in thyself so sweet and softly fair,
Within thine eyes ancestral Springs I trace;
So some wronged woman, in her baby's face
  May shuddering see its father's likeness there,
  While parted raptures thrill through her despair.

YOUTH AND NATURE.

Is this the sky, and this the very earth
  I had such pleasure in when I was young?
  And can this be the identical sea-song,
Heard once within the storm-cloud's awful girth
When a great storm from silence burst to birth,
  And winds to whom it seemed I did belong
  Made the keen blood in me run swift and strong
With irresistible, tempestuous mirth?
Are these the forests loved of old so well,
  Where on May nights enchanted music was?
  Are these the fields of soft, delicious grass,
These the old hills with secret things to tell?
O my dead youth, was this inevitable,
  That with thy passing, Nature, too, should pass?

A JULY DAY.

TO-DAY the sun has stedfast been and clear—
No wind has marred the spell of hushful heat,
But, with the twilight, comes a rush and beat
Of ghost-like wings; the sky turns grey and drear,
The trees are stricken with a sudden fear.
O wind forlorn, that sayeth nothing sweet,
With what foreboding message dost thou greet
The dearest month but one of all the year?

Ah, now it seems I catch the moan of seas
Whose boundaries are pale regions of dismay,
Where sad-eyed people wander without ease;
I see in thought that lamentable array,
And surely hear about the dying day
Recorded dooms and mournful prophecies.

A PARABLE.

A MAGIC circle holds me round, to-day—
The air is vital with the young, sweet Spring ;
In the fresh wind the leaves and grasses sing,
The songs of birds are blown from spray to spray,
The time is pure, and ardent, and how gay !
Now falls the saintly dusk ; low whispering
The gentle wind goes by with flagging wing
The sun to follow on his downward way.

Great quietude of moonlight holds the land ;
Now if one word I whisper to the air,
If one way turn, or even reach my hand,
The spell is broken ; and my Spring to scare
Comes Winter back, and shivering I stand,
Once more the old blast of his old winds to bear.

SONNETS ON SORROW.

I.

A CHILD, with mystic eyes and flowing hair,
  I saw her first, 'mid flowers that shared her grace;
  Though but a boy, I cried, "How fair a face!"
And, coming nearer, told her she was fair.
She faintly smiled, yet did not say "Forbear!"
  But seemed to take a pleasure in my praise.
  She led my steps through many a leafy place
And pointed where shy birds and sweet flowers were.

At length we stood upon a brooklet's brink—
  I seem to hear its sources babbling yet—
She gave me water from her hand to drink,
  The while her eyes upon its flow were set.
  "Thy name?" I asked; she whispered low,
      "Regret,"
Then faded, as the sun began to sink.

II.

We met again, as I foresaw we should;
Youth flooded all my veins, and she had grown
To woman's height, yet seemed a rose half blown.
Like sunset clouds that o'er a landscape brood
Her eyes were, that they might not be withstood,
And like the wind's voice when it takes the tone
Of pine trees was her voice. I cried, "My own!"—
And kneeling there I worshipped her and wooed.

O bitter marriage, though inevitable,
Ordained by Fate, who wrecks or saves our days!
Lo, the changed bride, no longer fair of face,
And in her eyes the very fires of hell!
"Thy name?" I cried; and these words hissing fell—
"Anguish—and madness come of my embrace."

III.

WHAT thing may be to come I cannot know.
  Her eyes have less of Hell in them, meanwhile;
  At times she almost smiles a ghastly smile,
I have in all things done her bidding so.
Chill are the rooms wherein no bright fires glow,
  Where no fair picture does the eye beguile;
  Once awful laughter shook the gloomy pile,
Unholy, riotous shapes, went to and fro.

There is no sound, now, in the house at all,
  Only outside the wind moans on, alway.
  My Lady Sorrow has no word to say,
Seems half content; for well she knows her thrall
Shall not escape from her; that should God call
  She would rise with him at the Judgment Day.

IN PRAISE OF SLEEP.

THERE is a Land where nightly I repair,
  At whose dim gate I put my cross aside,
  Stretch out my arms toward Rest as toward a bride,
And am withal assuaged. Ah, even there,
Beyond false hope, beyond the stress of prayer,
  Beyond the hurt and smart of broken pride,
  With no more hunger for sweet things denied,
My heart has rest and respite from despair.
O land of mystic shapes and languid pleasure—
  Waste field of poppies without track it seems—
  O scentless lilies by the voiceless streams
Where come my ghosts and dance a silent measure,
  Hold, my last joy now;—only in dear dreams
Give back to me, sometimes, my buried treasure.

MY LIFE.

To me my life seems as a haunted house,
  The ways and passages whereof are dumb,
  Up whose decaying stair no footsteps come;
Lo, this the hall hung with sere laurel boughs,
Where long years back came victors to carouse;
  But none of all that company went home;
  For scarce their lips had quaffed the bright wine's
    foam,
When sudden Death brake dank upon their brows.

Here in this lonely, ruined house I dwell,
While unseen fingers toll the chapel bell;
Sometimes the arras rustles, and I see
  A half-veiled figure through the twilight steal,
Which, when I follow, pauses suddenly
  Before the door whereon is set a seal.

HAUNTED ROOMS.

MUST this not be, whate'er the years disclose,
  When I and those in whom my heart has vent,
  From whose dear lives soul-light to mine is sent,
Lie at the last beneath where the grass grows,
Make one, in one interminable repose,
  Not knowing whence we came or whither went,
  Done with regret, with black presentiment
Of greater griefs, yet more victorious foes—

Must this not be that one then dwelling here,
  Where one man and his sorrows dwelt so long,
  Shall feel the pressure of a ghostly throng,
And shall upon some desolate midnight hear
  A sound more sad than is the pine-trees' song,
And thrill with great, inexplicable fear?

WORTH REMEMBRANCE.

OF me ye may say many a bitter thing,
  O Men, when I am gone, gone far away
  To that dim Land where shines no light of day.
Sharp was the bread for my soul's nourishing
Which Fate allowed, and bitter was the spring
  Of which I drank and maddened, even as they
  Who wild with thirst at sea will not delay,
But drink the brine and die of its sharp sting.

Not gentle was my war with Chance, and yet
  I borrowed no man's sword—alone I drew,
  And gave my slain fit burial out of view.
In secret places I and Sorrow met.
So, when you count my sins, do not forget
  To say I taxed not any one of you.

A LIFE.

HE walked 'midst shadows, and he nursed at heart
  A grief that set strange poison in his blood,
  He lived, and was of no man understood;
In all glad things that be he had no part,
And wearily he turned unto his art,
  But of his labour had he little good.
  Comfort he sought in cheerless solitude,
But visionary faces made him start.

Wrong things he did, was quick of thought and speech,
  For grievous sin had grievous punishment,
Missed love, missed Fame, both once within his reach,
  Nor might succeed in any high intent;
  And when he died had on his monument—
"All that Life taught him, Lord, let Death unteach."

MY LAND.

I WALK 'neath sunless skies; by flowerless ways
With failing feet and heavy heart I go.
Through leafless trees vague winds of twilight blow
A strange, still land it is; ghosts of old days
Rise up to meet me, a beloved, dead face
Emerges on my path; or sweet and low
The accents of some voice I used to know
Fall on my heart, where only sorrow stays.

My ghostly Land, wherethro', myself a ghost,
I journey ever toward that stranger strand
By which no ships from this world ever coast,
Ah, *there* shall I remember, still, my Land?
Nay, God—If any God indeed there be—
Grant me, in Death, release from Memory.

WARFARE WITH THE GODS.

THIS man was full of strength once, hope, and fire;
And when the gods derided him, he said,
"O Gods, your curse lies heavy on my head;
Against my peace I know that you conspire;
But, lo! I can defy you. Will ye tire
Yourselves with warfare? shall my soul fall dead
Because scant blessings on her head are shed?
Some things are still left dear to my desire,
And these shall give me courage in despite."
"Thou fool!" the gods laughed, and with wrong on wrong,
As seas come wave on wave when winds are strong,
They came against him, and laid waste his might,
Till, utterly humbled, prostrate in their sight,
He fell, and moaned, "My Masters, O, how long?"

A WISH.

I DO but ask a little time of peace
 Before the end of all. I crave no bliss ;
 I crave no love, nor fame, but only this—
On summer days to bask beneath old trees,
Or half asleep to lie by gentle seas,
 Hearing the waves that whisper ere they kiss,
 Then break and babble ; or, when twilight is,
And one by one the birds from singing cease,
Wander the patient, tranquil hills among,
 And languish in an exquisite regret,
And hear a sad but not discordant song
 Possess the air ; and when the sun is set,
Lie down with thankfulness to know, ere long,
 All things that ever were I shall forget.

A QUESTION.

If I had been in love with Life, had Death
  Seemed any ghastlier, more full of dread,
  Or I shrank more from thought of being dead,
Sightless and still, and in my lips no breath—
Night all about me, and the dust beneath?
  Not so, I think, for then I should have said—
  "I have been glad, though now I make my bed
Where dead folk lie, and never a word one saith."

Harder seems this—to die and leave the sun,
  And carry hence each unfulfilled desire.
    I heard one cry, "Come, where the feast is spread;"
But when I came the festival was done;
  Somewhile I shivered by the extinguished fire,
    And now retrace my steps uncomforted.

MAN'S DAYS.

FROM sorrow unto sorrow man progresses,
  If length of days be his, till, come at last,
  Nigh to that realm unknowable and vast,
Which hides the whole world's dead in its recesses,
Where iron night on every sleeper presses,
  In its strange neighbourhood he moves aghast;
  Remembering intermittently his past,
Lulled sometimes by a gentle ghost's caresses.

He moves down ways and by-ways listlessly,
  A traveller who, having paid his score,
  Knowing therewith he hath to do no more,
Waits till the ship already in sight be free
  To bear him back to his far, natal shore,
Back through the darkness and the awful sea.

DREAM MOONLIGHT.

DREAM moonlight, which for me sometimes makes
bright
And fair and wonderful the vales of sleep
Where spirits come in dreams to laugh or weep,
Is, more than that which floods the actual night,
A secret, subtle message to the sight.
Sometimes it falls upon a pale dream-deep,
Or fair untrodden fields no reapers reap,
Or some unscaled and inaccessible height.

Sometimes it falls 'twixt branches of dream-trees;
Then the fair light and shade divinely blend.
O fair dream moonlight, which dost give surcease
To this sore heart from memories that rend,
If death were but to languish in thy peace,
How could one stay and battle to the end?

BRIDAL EVE.

HALF robed, with gold hair drooped o'er shoulders white,
She sits as one entranced, with eyes that gaze
Upon the mirrored beauties of her face ;
And through the distances of dark and light
She hears faint music of the coming night ;
She hears the murmurs of receding days ;
Her future life is veiled in such a haze
As hides, on sultry morns, the sun from sight.

Upon the brink of imminent change she stands,
Glad, yet afraid to look beyond the verge ;
She starts, as at the touch of unseen hands ;
Love's music grows half anthem and half dirge.
Strange sounds and shadows round her spirit fall,
Yet to herself she stranger seems than all.

NO DEATH.

I SAW in dreams a mighty multitude—
Gathered, they seemed, from North, South, East and West,
And in their looks such horror was exprest
As must forever words of mine elude.
As if tranfixed by grief, some silent stood,
While others wildly smote upon the breast,
And cried out fearfully, "No rest, no rest!"
Some fled, as if by shapes unseen pursued.

Some laughed insanely. Others shrieking, said,
"To think but yesterday we might have died;
For then God had not thundered, 'Death is dead!'"
They gashed themselves till all with blood were red.
"Answer, O God; take back this curse!" they cried—
But "Death is dead," was all the voice replied.

Garden Secrets.

GARDEN SECRETS.

MY GARDEN.

O my Garden, full of roses,
Red as passion and as sweet,
Failing not when summer closes,
Lasting on through cold and heat!

O my Garden, full of lilies,
White as peace, and very tall,
In your midst my heart so still is
I can hear the least leaf fall!

O my Garden, full of singing
From the birds that house therein,
Sweet notes down the sweet day ringing
Till the nightingales begin!

THE ROSE AND THE WIND.

DAWN.

The Rose.

WHEN, think you, comes the Wind,
    The Wind that kisses me and is so kind?
Lo, how the Lily sleeps! her sleep is light.
Would I were like the Lily, pale and white!
Will the Wind come?

The Beech.

Perchance for thee too soon.

The Rose.

If not, how could I live until the noon?
What think you, Beech-tree, makes the Wind delay?
Why comes he not at breaking of the day?

The Beech.

Hush, child! and, like the Lily, go to sleep.

The Rose.

You know I cannot.

The Beech.

Nay, then, do not weep.

(*After a pause.*)

Thy lover comes ; be happy, now, O Rose !
He softly through my bending branches goes.
Soon he shall come, and thou shalt feel his kiss.

The Rose.

Already my flushed heart grows faint with bliss.
Love, I have longed for you through all the night.

The Wind.

And I to kiss your petals warm and bright.

The Rose.

Laugh round me, Love, and kiss me ; it is well.
Nay, have no fear ; the Lily will not tell.

MORNING.

The Rose.

'Twas dawn when first you came ; and now the sun
Shines brightly, and the dews of dawn are done.

'Tis well you take me so in your embrace,
But lay me back again into my place;
For I am worn, perhaps with bliss extreme.

The Wind.

Nay, you must wake, Love, from this childish dream.

The Rose.

'Tis you, Love, who seem changed; your laugh is loud,
And 'neath your stormy kiss my head is bowed.
O Love, O Wind, a space will not you spare?

The Wind.

Not while your petals are so soft and fair.

The Rose.

My buds are blind with leaves, they cannot see;
O Love, O Wind, wilt thou not pity me?

EVENING.

The Beech.

O Wind! a word with you before you pass:
What did you to the Rose, that on the grass
Broken she lies, and pale, who loved you so?

The Wind.

Roses must live and love, and winds must blow.

THE DISPUTE.

The Grass.

I FELT upon me, as she passed, her feet.

The Beech.

'Neath my green shade she sheltered in the heat.

A Rose.

She plucked me as she passed, and in her breast
Wore me, and I was to her beauty prest.

The Wind.

And now ye lie neglected, withering fast;
And the Grass withers too; and when have past
These golden summer days, O Beech, no more
She'll sit beneath thy shade. But I endure,
To kiss her when I will. So, more than ye,
Am I made blest in my felicity.

WHAT THE ROSE SAW.

The Rose.

O LILY sweet! I saw a pleasant sight.

The Lily.

Where saw you it, and when?

The Rose.

Here, when the Night
Lay calmly over all and covered us,
And no wind blew, however tremulous,
I heard afar the light fall of *her* feet,
And murmur of her raiment soft and sweet.

The Lily.

What said she to thee when she came anear?

The Rose.

No word; but o'er me bent till I could hear
The beating of her heart, and feel her blood
Swell to a blossom that which was a bud.

Alas! I have no words to tell the bliss
When on my trembling petals fell her kiss;
Sweeter than soft rain falling after heat,
Or dew at dawn, was that kiss, soft and sweet.
Then fell another shadow on the ground,
And for a little space there was no sound.
I knew who stood beside her, saw his face
Shining and happy in that happy place;
I knew not what they said; but this I know,
They kissed and passed: where think you they did
go?

THE GARDEN'S LOSS.

A Lily.

HE will not speak to us again;
No more the sudden summer rain
Will fall from off his trembling leaves:
Even the scentless Tulip grieves.
Ah me! the loud noise of that night,
And that fierce blaze of blinding light
That slew him in the midst of bliss—
Reach out, O Rose! and let us kiss.

The Rose.

He was a friend to all indeed;
Even the wild, unlovely Weed
Loved him and clove unto his root:
When next winds blow he shall be mute.

The Lily.

He was the noblest of all trees.

A Tulip.

Your sorrow cannot bring you ease.

The Lily.

Still we *must* mourn so great a one.

The Rose.

I would the summer-time were done !
The birds we loved sang in his boughs,
And in his branches made their house.
All graciously he bowed and swayed ;
And when of winds we were afraid,
How tenderly his boughs he moved,—
A loving tree, and well beloved.

An Elm.

He was a noble tree and vast ;
His branches revelled in the blast :
I always took him for our king.
Yet better that he was so slain,
In midst of his loved wind and rain,
Than some sharp axe should lay him low.

The Rose.

Better ! but now I only know
He shall not speak again to me—
Nor, Lily, shall he speak to thee.

BEFORE AND AFTER FLOWERING.

BEFORE.

First Violet.

Lo, here how warm and dark and still it is!
Sister, lean close to me, that we may kiss.
Here we go rising, rising; but to where?

Second Violet.

Indeed I cannot tell, nor do I care,
It is so warm and pleasant here. But hark!
What strangest sound was that above the dark?

First Violet.

As if our sisters all together sang,—
Seemed it not so?

Second Violet.

More loud than that it rang;
And louder still it rings, and seems more near.
Oh, I am shaken through and through with fear!

Now in some deadly grip I seem confined !—
Farewell, my sister ! Rise and follow and find.

First Violet.

From how far off those last words seemed to fall !
Gone where she will not answer when I call !
How lost ? How gone ? Alas ! this sound above me :
" Poor little Violet, left with none to love thee ! "
And now it seems I break against that sound !
What bitter pain is this that binds me round ?
This pain I press into ? Where have I come ?

AFTER.

A Coocus.

Welcome, dear sisters, to our fairy home !
They call this Garden, and the time is Spring.
Like you, I have felt the pain of flowering ;
But oh ! the wonder and the deep delight
It was to stand here, in the broad sunlight,
And feel the wind flow round me cool and kind ;
To hear the singing of the leaves the wind
Goes hurrying through ; to see the mighty trees,
Where every day the blossoming buds increase !

At evening, when the shining sun goes in,
The gentler lights we see, and dews begin,
And all is still beneath the quiet sky,
Save sometimes for the wind's low lullaby.

First Tree.

Poor little flowers!

Second Tree.

What would you prate of now?

First Tree.

They have not heard; I will keep still. Speak low.

First Violet.

The trees bend to each other lovingly.

Crocus.

Daily they talk of fairer things to be.
Great talk they make about the coming Rose,
The very fairest flower, they say, that blows,
Such scent she hath; her leaves are red, they say,
And fold her round in some divine, sweet way.

First Violet.

Would she were come, that for ourselves we might
Have pleasure in this wonder of delight!

Crocus.

Here comes the laughing, dancing, hurrying rain:
How all the trees laugh at the wind's light strain!

First Violet.

We are so near the earth, the wind goes by
And hurts us not; but if we stood up high,
Like trees, then should we soon be blown away.

Second Violet.

Nay; were it so, we should be strong as they.

Crocus.

I often think how nice to be a tree;
Why, sometimes in their boughs the stars I see.

First Violet.

Have you seen that?

Crocus.

I have, and so shall you.
But hush! I feel the coming of the dew.

NIGHT.

Second Violet.

How bright it is! the trees how still they are!

Crocus.

I never saw before so bright a star
As that which stands and shines just over us.

First Violet (after a pause).

My leaves feel strange and very tremulous.

Crocus and Second Violet together.

And mine, and mine!

First Violet.

O, warm, kind Sun, appear!

Crocus.

I would the stars were gone, and day were here!

JUST BEFORE DAWN.

First Violet.

Sisters! No answer, sisters? Why so still?

One Tree to Another.

Poor little Violet, calling through the chill
Of this new frost which did her sister slay,
In which she must herself, too, pass away!

Nay, pretty Violet, be not so dismayed ;
Sleep only on your sisters sweet is laid.

First Violet.

No pleasant Wind about the garden goes,—
Perchance the Wind has gone to bring the Rose.
O sisters ! surely now your sleep is done.
I would we had not looked upon the sun.
My leaves are stiff with pain.   O cruel night !
And through my root some sharp thing seems to bite.
Ah me ! what pain, what coming change is this ?

(*She dies.*)

First Tree.

So endeth many a Violet's dream of bliss.

THE ROSE'S DREAM.

I.

O SISTERS! when last night so well you slept,
I could not sleep; but through the silent air
I looked upon the white moon, shining where
No scent of any rose can reach, I know.
And as I looked adown the path there crept
A little trembling, restless Wind, and lo!
As near it came, I said: "O little Breeze
That hast no strength wherewith to stir the trees!
What dost thou in this place?" It only sighed,
And paused a little ere it thus replied:—

II.

"I am the Wind that comes before the rain
Which, even now, bears onward from the west,—
The rain that is as sweet to you as rest.
When all the air about the day lies dead,
And the incessant sunlight grows a pain,
Then by the cool rain are you comforted.

O happy Rose, that shall not live to see
This summer garden altered utterly,
You know not of the days of snow and ice,
Nor know the look of wild and wintry skies."

III.

Then passed the Wind; but left me very sad,
For I began to think of days to come,
Wherein the sun should fail and birds grow dumb,
And how this garden then should look, indeed.
And as I thought of all, such fear I had
I cried to you, asleep, though none would heed.
And so I wept, though none might see me weep,
Till came the Wind again, and bade me sleep,
And sang me such a small, sweet song that soon
I fell asleep while looking on the moon.

IV.

And as I slept I dreamed a fearful dream.
It seemed to me that I was standing here:
The sky was sunless, and I saw anear
All you, my sisters, lying dead and crushed.
I could not hear the music of the stream
That runs hard by, when suddenly there rushed
A giant Wind adown the garden walk,
And all the great old Trees began to talk

And cried "What does the Rose here? Bid her go,
Lest buried she should be in coming snow."

V.

I strove to move away, but all in vain;
And, flying, as it passed me cried the Wind:
"O foolish little Rose, and art thou blind?
Dost thou not see the snow is coming fast?"
And all the swaying Trees cried out again:
"O foolish Rose, to tarry till the last!
Then came a sudden whirl, a mighty noise,
As every tree that lives had found a voice;
And I was borne away, and lifted high
As birds that dart in summer through the sky.

VI.

And then the great Wind fell away; and so
I felt that I was whirling down and down,
Past trees that strove, with branches bare and brown,
To catch me as I fell; and all they cried:
"She must be buried in the cold deep snow;
Ah, would she had like other roses died!"
Then, as I thought to drop, I woke to find
The cool rain falling on me, and the Wind
Singing a rainy song among the trees,
Wherein the birds were building at their ease.

VII.

First Flower.

A fearful dream indeed, and such an one
As well may make you sad for days to come.

Second Flower.

A sad, strange dream !

The Rose.

Why is the Lily dumb ?

The Lily.

Too sad the dream for me to speak about !

The Rose.

I fear this night the setting of the sun.

A Tree.

Nay, when the sun goes in, the stars come out.
You shall not dream, Rose, such a dream again ;
Forget it now in listening to the rain.

The Rose.

I would the Wind had never talked to me
Of things that I shall never live to see.

THE FLOWER AND THE HAND.

I.

JUST AFTER NIGHTFALL.

I HEARD a whisper of roses,
  And light white Lilies laugh out :
"Ah ! sweet when the evening closes,
  And stars come looking about ;
How cool and good it is to stand,
Nor fear at all the gathering hand !"

II.

"Would I were red !" cried a White Rose.
  "Would I were white !" cried a red one ;
"No longer the light Wind blows,
  He went with the dear, dead Sun.
Here we forever seem to stay ;
And yet a Sun dies every day."

III.

A Lily.

"The Sun is not dead, but sleeping,
  And each day the same Sun wakes;
But when stars their watch are keeping,
  Then a time of rest he takes."

Many Roses together.

"How very wise these Lilies are!
They must have heard Sun talk with Star!"

IV.

First Rose.

"Pray, then, can you tell us, Lilies,
  Where slumbers the Wind at night,
When the Garden all round so still is,
  And brimmed with the Moon's pale light?"

A Lily.

"In branches of great trees he rests."

Second Rose.

"Not so; they are too full of nests."

First Rose.

"*I* think he sleeps where the grass is ;
He there would have room to lie.
The white Moon over him passes ;
He wakes with the dawning Sky."

Many Lilies together.

"How very wise these Roses seem,
Who think they know, and only dream !"

VI.

First Rose.

"What haps to a gathered flower ?"

Second Rose.

"Nay, sister, now who can tell ?
Not one comes back for an hour,
To say it is ill or well.
I would with such an one confer,
To know what strange things chanced to her."

VII.

First Rose.

" Hush ! hush ! now the Wind is waking—
  Or *is* it the Wind I hear ?
My leaves are thrilling and shaking—
  Good-bye ; I am gathered, my dear !
Now, whether for my bliss or woe,
I shall know what the plucked flowers know ! "

GARDEN FAIRIES.

KEEN was the air, the sky was very light,
Soft with shed snow my garden was, and white;
And walking there, I heard upon the night
Sudden sound of little voices,—
Just the prettiest of noises.

It was the strangest, subtlest, sweetest sound;
It seemed above me, seemed upon the ground,
Then swiftly seemed to eddy round and round;
Till I said: "To-night the air is
Surely full of garden fairies."

And all at once it seemed I grew aware
That little shining presences were there,
White shapes and red shapes danced upon the air;
Then a deal of silver laughter;
And such singing followed after

As none of you, I think, have ever heard,
More soft it was than note of any bird,—
Note after note, most exquisitely deferred,

Soft as dew-drops when they settle
In a fair flower's open petal.

"What are these fairies?" to myself I said;
For answer, then, as from a garden's bed,
On the cold air, a sudden scent was shed,—
Scent of lilies, scent of roses,
Scent of Summer's sweetest posies.

And said a small sweet voice within my ear:
"We flowers that sleep through winter, once a year
Are by our flower queen let to visit here,
That this fact may duly flout us—
Gardens can look fair without us.

"A very little time we have to play;
Then must we go, oh? very far away,
And sleep again for many a long, long day,
Till the glad birds sing above us,
And the warm Sun comes to love us.

"Hark what the roses sing, now, as we go!"
Then very sweet and soft, and very low,—
A dream of sound across the garden snow,—
Came the sound of Roses singing
To the Lily-bells' faint ringing.

ROSE'S SONG.

"Softly sinking through the snow,
To our winter rest we go;
Underneath the snow to house
Till the birds be in the boughs,
And the boughs with leaves be fair,
And the sun shine everywhere.
Softly through the snow we settle,
Little Snowdrops press each petal.
Oh! the snow is kind and white,
Soft it is, and very light;
Soon we shall be where no light is,
But where sleep is, and where night is,—
Sleep of every wind unshaken
Till our summer bids us waken."

Then toward some far-off goal that singing drew,
Then altogether ceased; more steely blue
The blue stars shone; but in my spirit grew
Hope of summer, love of roses,
Certainty that sorrow closes.

SUMMER CHANGES.

SANG the Lily and sang the Rose,
Out of the heart of my garden close :
  " O joy, O joy of the summer tide ! "
Sang the Wind, as it moved above them :
" Roses were sent for the Sun to love them,
  Dear little buds, in the leaves that hide ! "

Sang the Trees, as they rustled together :
" O the joy of the summer weather !
  Roses and Lilies, how do you fare ? "
Sang the Red Rose, and sang the White :
" Glad we are of the Sun's large light,
  And the songs of the birds that dart through
    the air."

Lily, and Rose, and tall green Tree,
Swaying boughs where the bright birds be,
  Thrilled by music, and thrilled by wings,
How glad they were on that summer day !
Little they recked of cold skies and grey,
  Or the dreary dirge that a Storm-Wind sings !

Golden butterflies gleam in the sun,
Laugh at the flowers, and kiss each one;
  And great bees come, with their sleepy tune,
To sip their honey and circle round;
And the flowers are lulled by that drowsy sound,
  And fall asleep in the heart of the noon.

A small white cloud in a sky of blue:
Roses and Lilies, what will they do?
  For a wind springs up and sings in the trees.
Down comes the rain; the garden's awake:
Roses and Lilies begin to quake,
  That were rocked to sleep by the gentle breeze.

Ah, Roses and Lilies! Each delicate petal
The wind and the rain with fear unsettle—
  This way and that way the tall trees sway:
But the wind goes by, and the rain stops soon,
And smiles again the face of the noon,
  And the flowers grow glad in the sun's warm ray.

Sing, my Lilies, and sing, my Roses,
With never a dream that the summer closes.
  But the Trees are old; and I fancy they tell,
Each unto each, how the summer flies:
They remember the last year's wintry skies;
  But that summer returns the Trees know well.

THE LONELY ROSE.

"To a heaven far away
  Went the Red Rose when she died."
So I heard the White Rose say,
  As she swayed from side to side
    In the chill October blast.
    In the garden leaves fall fast;
    This of roses is the last:

Said the White Rose: "O my Red Rose!
  O my Rose so fair to see!
When, like thee, I am a dead rose,
  Shall *I* in that heaven be?"
    Oh, the dread October blast!
    In the garden leaves fall fast;
    This of roses is the last.

"From that heavenly place, last night,
  To me in a dream she came,
Stood there in the pale moonlight;
  And she seemed, my Rose, the same."

Oh, the bleak October blast!
In the garden leaves fall fast;
This of roses is the last.

"Only it may be, perchance,
That her leaves were redder grown,
And they seemed to thrill and dance,
As by gentler breezes blown."
O, the sad October blast!
In the garden leaves fall fast;
This of roses is the last.

"And she told me, sweetly singing,
Of that heavenly place afar,
Where the air with song is ringing,
Where the souls of blossoms are."
Hark, the wild October blast!
In the garden leaves fall fast;
This of roses is the last.

"And she bade me not to fail her,
Nor to lose my heart for fear,
When I saw the skies turn paler
With the sickness of the year,—
I should be beyond the blast,
And the dead leaves falling fast,
In that heavenly place at last."

ROSES AND THE NIGHTINGALE.

IN my garden it is night-time,
But a still time and a bright time;
For the moon rains down her splendour,
  And my garden feels the wonder
  Of the spell which it lies under
In that light so soft and tender.

While the moon her watch is keeping,
All the Blossoms here are sleeping.
And the Roses sigh for dreaming
  Of the bees that love to love them
  When the warm sun shines above them
And the butterflies pass gleaming.

Could one follow Rose's fancies
When the night the garden trances,
Oh, what fair things we should chance on!
  For to Lilies and to Roses,
  As to us, soft sleep discloses
What the waking may not glance on.

But hark ! now across the moonlight,
Through the warmness of the June night,
From the tall Trees' listening branches,
  Comes the sound, sustained and holy,
  Of the passionate melancholy,
Of a wound which singing stanches.

Oh, the ecstasy of sorrow
Which the music seems to borrow
From the thought of some past lover
  Who loved vainly all his lifetime,
  Till death ended peace and strife-time,
And the darkness clothed him over !

Oh, the passionate, sweet singing,
Aching, gushing, throbbing, ringing,
Dying in divine, soft closes,
  Recommencing, waxing stronger,
  Sweet notes, ever sweeter, longer,
Till the singing wakes the Roses !

Quoth the Roses to the singer :
"Oh, thou dearest music-bringer,
Now our sleep so sweetly endeth,
  Tell us why *thy* song so sad seems,
  When the air is full of glad dreams,
And the bright moon o'er us bendeth."

Sang the Singer to the Roses :
" Love for you my song discloses ;
Hence the note of grief it borrows."
  Quoth the Roses : "Love means pleasure."
  Quoth the Singer : "Love's best measure
Is its pure attendant sorrows."

THY GARDEN.

I.

PURE moonlight in thy garden, sweet, to-night,
Pure moonlight in thy garden, and the breath
Of fragrant roses. O my heart's delight!
Wed thou with Love, but I will wed with Death!

Peace in thy garden, and the passionate song
Of some last nightingale that sings in June!
Thy dreams with promises of love are strong,
And all thy life is set to one sweet tune.

Love wandering round thy garden, O my sweet!
Love walking through thy garden in the night;
Far off I feel his wings, I hear his feet,
I see the eyes that set the world alight.

My sad heart in thy garden strays alone,
My heart among all hearts companionless;
Between the roses and the lilies thrown,
It finds thy garden but a wilderness.

Great quiet in thy garden, now the song
Of that last nightingale has died away!
Here jangling city chimes the silence wrong,
But in thy garden perfect rest has sway.

Dawn in thy garden, with the faintest sound,—
Uncertain, tremulous, awaking birds,—
Dawn in thy garden, and from meadows round,
The sudden lowing of expectant herds.

Light in thy garden, faint and sweet and pure;
Dim noise of birds from every bush and tree;
Rumours of song the stars may not endure;
A rain that falls and ceases suddenly.

Morn in thy garden,—bright and keen and strong!
Love calls thee, from thy garden, to awake;
Morn in thy garden, with the articulate song
Of birds that sing for love and warm light's sake.

II.

Wind in thy garden to-night, my Love,
Wind in thy garden and rain;
A sound of storm in the shaken grove,
And cries as of spirits in pain!

If there's wind in thy garden outside,
  And troublous darkness, dear,
What carest thou, an elected bride,
  And the bridal hour so near?

All things come to an end, my sweet,—
  Life, and the pleasure in living;
The years run swiftly with agile feet,
  The years that are taking and giving.

Soon shalt thou have thy bliss supreme,
  And soon shall it pass away;
So turn thyself to thy rest and dream,
  Nor heed what the mad winds say.

III.

Snow in thy garden, falling thick and fast,
  Snow in thy garden, where the grass shall be!
What dreams to-night? Thy dreaming nights are past;
  Thou hast no glad or grievous memory.

Love in thy garden boweth down his head,
  His tears are falling on the wind-piled snow;
He takes no heed of life, now thou art dead,
  He recks not how the seasons come or go.

Death in thy garden! In the violent air
  That sweeps thy radiant garden thou art still;
For thee is no more rapture or despair,
  And Love and Death of thee have had their will.

Night in thy garden, white with snow and sleet;
  Night rushing on with wind and storm toward
    day,—
Alas! thy garden holdeth nothing sweet,
  Nor sweet can come again, and *Thou* away.

WIND-GARDENS.

Midway between earth and sky,
There the wild wind-gardens lie,—
Tossing gardens, secret bowers,
Full of songs and full of flowers,
Wafting down to us below
Such a fragrance as we know
Never yet had lily or rose
That our fairest garden knows.

Oh, these gardens dear and far
Where the wild wind-fairies are!—
Though we see not, we can hearken
To them when the spring skies darken,
Singing clearly, singing purely
Songs of far-off Elf-land, surely,
And they pluck the wild-wind posies,
Lilies, violets, and roses.

Each to each the sweet buds flinging,
Fostering, tending them, and singing.
The sweet scent, like angels' pity,
Finds us, even in the city,

Where we, toiling, seek as treasures
Dull earth's disenchanting pleasures.
Oh, the gales, with wind-flowers laden,
Flowers that no mortal maiden

In her breast shall ever wear!
Flowers to wreathe Titania's hair,
And to strew her happy way with,
When she marries some wind-fay with!
O wind-gardens! where such songs are,
And of flowers such happy throngs are,
Though your paths I may not see,
Well I know how fair they be.

FLOWER FAIRIES.

FLOWER fairies have you found them,
  When the summer's dusk is falling,
With the glow-worms all around them,
  Have you heard them softly calling?

Calling through your garden spaces
  Notes like fairy bells set ringing,
Heard from out enchanted places
  Whence the fairy bees come winging?

Silent stand they through the moonlight,
  In their flower shapes fair and quiet,
But they quit them in the moonlight,
  In its beams to sing and riot.

I have heard them, *I* have seen them,
  From their petals light-like raying,
And the trees would fain have been them,
  The great trees too old for playing.

Hundreds of them altogether,
  Flashing flocks of flying fairies,
Crowding through the summer weather,
  Seeking where the coolest air is.

And they tell the trees that know them,
As upon their bows they hover,
Of the things that chance below them,
How the rose has a new lover.

And the roses laugh protesting
That the lilies are as fickle;
Then they look where birds are nesting,
And their feathers softly tickle.

Then away they all go sweeping,
Having had their fill of gladness,
But the trees, their night-watch keeping,
Feel a tender loving sadness.

For *they* know of bleak December,
When each bough to pain left bare is,
When they only shall remember
Those bright visitings of fairies;

When the roses and the lilies
Shall be gone, to come back never,
To a land where all so still is,
That they sleep and sleep for ever.

Poems and Ballads

from "Wind-Voices."

POEMS AND BALLADS FROM "WIND VOICES."

PURE SOULS.

PURE souls that watch above me from afar
  To whom as to the stars I raise my eyes,
  Draw me to your large skies,
Where God and quiet are.

Love's mouth is rose-red, and his voice is sweet,
  His feet are winged, his eyes are as clear fire;
  But I have no desire
To follow his winged feet.

Friendships may change, or friends may pass away,
  And Fame's a bride that men soon weary of;
  Since rest is not with Love,
No joy that is may stay.

But they whose lives are pure, whose hearts are high—
Those shining spirits by the world untamed,
May, at the end, unshamed,
Look on their days gone by.

O pure, strong souls, so star-like, calm, and bright,
If even I before the end might feel,
Through quiet pulses, steal
Your pureness—with purged sight

I might Spring's gracious work behold once more,
Might hear, as once I heard, long, long ago,
Great waters ebb and flow,
Might smell the rose of yore,

Might comprehend the winds and clouds again,
The saintly, peaceful moonlight hallowing all,
The scent of leaves that fall,
The Autumn's tender pain.

Ah, this, I fear, shall never chance to me,
And though I cannot shape the life I would,
It surely still is good
To look where such lives be.

AT PARTING.

I PUT my flower of song into thy hand,
And turn my eyes away—
It is a flower from a most desolate land,
Barren of sun and day,
Even this life of mine.
As two who meet upon a foreign strand,
'Twas mine with thee to stay—
I put this flower of song into thy hand
And turn my eyes away,
And look where no lights shine.

By phantom wings this desolate air seems fanned,
Where sky and sea show grey—
I put my flower of song into thy hand
And turn my eyes away,
But to no other shrine.
My hopes are like a little Christian band
The heathen came to slay—
I put this flower of song into thy hand
And turn my eyes away—
Keep thou the song in sign.

Some day, it may be, thou by me shalt stand
When no word my lips say,
And, holding then this song-flower in thy hand,
Shalt turn thine eyes away,
And drop pure tears divine.
We part at Fate's inexorable command,
We part to meet no day—
I put my flower of song into thy hand,
And turn my eyes away—
These eyes that burn and pine.

Thy way leads summerwards, thy paths are spanned
By boughs where spring winds play—
I put my flower of song into thy hand
And turn my eyes away
To Life's dark boundary line.
Fair are thy groves, thy fields lie bright and bland,
Where evil has no sway—
I put my flower of song into thy hand
And turn my eyes away
To meet Fate's eyes, malign.

Sometimes, when twilight holds and fills the land,
And glad souls are less gay,

Take thou this song-flower in thy tender hand
Nor turn thine eyes away,
There in the day's decline.
My life lies dark before me—all unplanned—
Loud winds assail the day—
I leave my song-flower folded in thy hand,
And turn my eyes away,
And turn my life from thine.

A BALLAD OF BRAVE WOMEN.

Off Swansea—January 27, 1883.

With hiss and thunder and inner boom,
White through the darkness the great waves loom,
And charge the rocks with the shock of doom.

A second sea is the hurricane's blast;
Its viewless billows are loud and vast,
By their strength great trees are uptorn, downcast.

To-night falls many a goodly tree,
As many a ship, through the raging sea,
Shall go with the strange sea-things to be.

At times, through the hurry of clouds, the moon
Looks out aghast; but her face right soon
Is hidden again, and she seems to swoon.

Oh, the wind-waves, and oh, the sea-waves,
The gulfs of wind, and sea-gulfs for graves!
Fast through the air how She flies and raves—

Raves with a magical, mad delight,
The viewless Spirit of the storm of the night,
Heart of the wind, and soul of his might.

Hark to the voice which shouts from the sea,
The voice of a fiendish revelry !
For the unseen hunters are out, and flee

Over the crests of the roaring deep,
Or they climb the waves that are wild and steep,
Or right through the heart of their light they leap.

Roar of the wind and roar of the waves,
And song and clamour of sea-filled caves !
What ship to-night such a tempest braves ?

Yet see, ah, see, how a snake of light
Goes hissing and writhing up all the night !
While the cry, "Going down !" through the winds' mad might—

Through the roar of the winds and the waves together—
Is sent this way by the shrieking weather ;
But to help on such night were a vain endeavour.

See ! a glare of torches, and married and single,
Men and women confusedly mingle—
You can hear the rush of their feet down the shingle.

O, salt and keen is the spray in their faces;
From the strength of the wind they reel in their paces,
Catch hands to steady them there in their places.

How would a boat in such seas behave?
But the lifeboat—the lifeboat—the lifeboat will save!
She is manned, with her crew of strong fellows, and
brave.

See! They ride on the heights, in the deep valleys dip,
Until, with a cry which the winds outstrip,
Their boat is hurled on the sinking ship.

Its side is gored, for the sea to have way through—
"It is over!" they cried. "We have done all men
may do!
Yet there's one chance left!" and themselves they threw

Right into the wrath of the sea and the wind.
It rages all round them, before and behind;
Their ears are deafened; their eyes are blind.

There in the middlemost hell of the night,
Yea, in the innermost heart of the fight,
They strain and they struggle with all their might—

With never a pause, while God's mercy they cry on;
Their teeth are set, their muscles are iron—
Each man has the heart and the thews of a lion.

Wave spurns them to wave. They may do it! Who
knows?
For shoreward the great tide towering goes,
And shoreward the great wind thundering blows.

But, no! See that wave, like a Fate bearing on!
It breaks them and passes. Two swimmers alone
Are seen mid the waves, and their strength is nigh gone.

Quoth three soldiers on shore, "They must give up all
hope.
Neither swimmer nor boat with such surges could cope,
Nor could one stand steady to cast a rope.

"For he who would cast it must stand hip-high
In the trough of the sea, and be thrown thereby
On his face, never more to behold the sky."

But a woman stept out from those gathered there,
And she said, "My life for their lives will I dare.
I pray for strength. God will hear my prayer."

And the light of her soul her eyes shone through,
But the men they jeered, and they cried, "Go to!
Can a woman do what we dare not do?"

Spake another woman—"I, too! We twain
Will do our best, striving might and main,
And if what we do shall be done in vain,

"And the great sea have us to hold and hide,
It were surely better thus to have died
Than to live as *these* live. Haste! haste!" she cried.

They seized a rope, and with no word more,
Fearless of death, down the steep of the shore,
They dashed right into the light and the roar

Of the giant waves, which sprang on them there,
As a beast on prey may spring from his lair,
While the roar of his triumph makes deaf the air.

Oh, loud is the Death they hurry to meet;
The stones slip shrieking from under their feet;
They stagger, but fall not. Beat, mad billows, beat!

They raise their arms, with their soul's strength
quivering—
They pause—"Will it reach?" Then they shout and
fling;
And straight as a stone driven forth by a sling,

Driven far afield by a master hand,
The rope whizzes out from the seething strand.
A shout—"It is caught! Now for land, for land!"

A crash like thunder! They drop to their knees,
But they keep their hold in the under seas.
They rise. Pull, pull! nor falter, nor cease.

The strength of ten men have these women to-night,
And they shout with the rapturous sense of their might—
They shout as men shout when they revel in fight.

They reel, but they fall not. The rope winds in, fast;
Then a shout, a near shout, answers their shout at last—
"That will do! We touch ground." God, the danger
is past!

They turn them, then, from the raging water
With the two they have snatched from its lust of slaughter;
But their feet flag now, and their breath comes shorter.

Hardly they hear in their sea-dinned ears
The sound of sobs, or the sound of cheers;
Their eyes are drowned, but not drowned with tears.

When deeds of valour Coast vaunts over Coast,
As to which proved bravest, and which did most,
Two Swansea women shall be my toast.

ESTRANGED.

SOME day she will come back, my poor lost dove—
My dove with the warm breast and eager eyes!
How did I fail toward her, my passionate love?
Where was the flaw? since flaw there must have been,
Or surely she had stayed with me, my queen.
Her heart was full of inarticulate cries,
Which my heart failed to catch; and yet she strove
To cleave to me—ah, how she must have striven,
Praying, perchance, ofttimes for strength from Heaven!
But no strength came; and so, one fatal day,
Despairing of all help, she went away.

And there her half-completed portrait stands—
The fresh young face, and grey eyes brimmed with
light;
I painted her with flowers in her hands,
Because she always seemed so bright and good.
I never thought the studio's solitude
Would hurt her, anyway. I thought the sight
Of painted forms and unfamiliar lands

Would be enough for her. She was too mild,
Too patient with my painter's life, poor child!
Had she complained at all, by look or tone,
Had she but said, "I seem too much alone,

"I grow half fearful of these painted eyes,
That never change, but, full of sad reproof,
Haunt me and watch me; and these Southern skies
Reflected in deep streams; and that dark boat
From which a girl with bare, sweet breast and throat
Droops, willow like, and dreams of life and love;
And that youth's dying face, which never dies;
And then, again, that picture of Christ there,
Christ fallen in an agony of prayer,
And His disciples near Him, stern and dumb,
Like men who know the fated hour is come."

Had she said thus, and added, "Take me, dear,
Outside of these sad faces; let me stand
Once more within life's shallows, and there hear
Light laughter of the surf upon the beach,
For here the very sea is without speech,
So still it is, and far away from land;
I want life's little joys; this atmosphere
Oppresses me; I cannot breathe in it;
The light that lights your life leaves mine unlit"—

I should have answered tenderly, and sought
To carry out, in all, her slightest thought.

She knew I loved her, through those winter days;
Did it not comfort her at all, my love?
It was such joy to look upon her face,
I sat for hours, content to be quite still,
Feeling her warm, bright breathing beauty fill
My soul and brain; fearful lest she should move,
And speak, or go; but when she met my gaze
I turned away, as if I had done wrong
In looking on her loveliness so long.
I rarely kissed her, rarely took her hand;
And now I think she did not understand.

Perchance she thought my love was passionless—
Wanted what I withheld, yet longed to give;
She did not know my silence a caress—
All passion was by reverence controlled—
And so she deemed my ways of love were cold.
Ah me! the lonely life she had to live,
And I knew nothing of its loneliness.
Here was a nature quick to give and take,
A nature to be broken and to break;
She loved confiding valleys, sun-kissed rills,
But saddened at the solemn peace of hills.

All things had been so different had I known
Her nature then as now; and yet, and yet,
If she came in as I sit here alone,
The April twilight failing through the room,
And all the pictures lapsing into gloom,—
Came in, knelt down, and prayed me to forget,
Forgive her, and reclaim her for my own,
I should be glad, and draw her to my heart,
And kiss the rising tears away, and part
The sweet hair back, and fold her to my side;
Yet leave, perchance, the want unsatisfied.

But ah! she comes not. I must wait and bear;
Live on, and serve my art as best I may.
If I can catch the colour of her hair,
And the neck's poise, and set beneath her name,
Shall not her loveliness have deathless fame?
O help me, Art, upon my difficult way!
Now lights shine out along the London square,
O dreary place! where no joy comes at all.
There! I must turn the easel to the wall,
I cannot bear her face as yet—O Love!
O wounded of my hands! my wounded dove!

THE OLD CHURCHYARD OF BONCHURCH.

[This old churchyard has been for many years slipping toward the sea, which it is expected will ultimately engulf it.]

THE churchyard leans to the sea with its dead—
It leans to the sea with its dead so long.
Do they hear, I wonder, the first bird's song,
When the winter's anger is all but fled,
The high, sweet voice of the west wind,
The fall of the warm, soft rain,
When the second month of the year
Puts heart in the earth again?

Do they hear, through the glad April weather,
The green grasses waving above them?
Do they think there are none left to love them,
They have lain for so long there, together?
Do they hear the note of the cuckoo,
The cry of gulls on the wing,
The laughter of winds and waters,
The feet of the dancing Spring?

Do they feel the old land slipping seaward,
The old land, with its hills and its graves,
As they gradually slide to the waves
With the wind blowing on them from leeward?
Do they know of the change that awaits them,
The sepulchre vast and strange?
Do they long for days to go over,
And bring that miraculous change?

Or they love, perhaps, their night with no moonlight,
With no starlight, no dawn to its gloom,
And they sigh—"'Neath the snow, or the bloom
Of the wild things that wave from our night,
We are warm, through winter and summer;
We hear the winds blow, and say—
'The storm-wind blows over our heads,
But we, here, are out of its way.'"

Do they mumble low, one to another,
With a sense that the waters that thunder
Shall ingather them all, draw them under,
"Ah! how long to our moving, brother?
How long shall we quietly rest here,
In graves of darkness and ease?
The waves, even now, may be on us,
To draw us down under the seas!"

Do they think 'twill be cold when the waters
That they love not, that neither can love them,
Shall eternally thunder above them?
Have they dread of the sea's shining daughters,
That people the bright sea-regions
And play with the young sea-kings?
Have they dread of their cold embraces,
And dread of all strange sea-things?

But their dread or their joy—it is bootless:
They shall pass from the breast of their mother;
They shall lie low, dead brother by brother,
In a place that is radiant and fruitless,
And the folk that sail over their heads
In violent weather
Shall come down to them, haply, and all
They shall lie there, together.

JUST ASLEEP.

For a space the shadows lift now,
  Now that we are nearly met;
By what windings shall we drift now,
  To what shore our keel be set?
Dearest Sleep, so long denied me,
To what regions wilt thou guide me?

Let us leave behind old sorrow,
  In the room where Death has been;
Let it bide there till to-morrow,
  Let it stalk of no man seen.
Though to-morrow it will find me,
Yet to-night 'twill stay behind me.

Yes, to-morrow, iron-hearted
  As the hearts of all my days,
We shall be no longer parted,
  No more travelling by strange ways;
But together, whom forever
Death alone can really sever.

Wilt thou show me ſair dream spaces
  Where my dead ones do not seem
Dead with dust upon their ſaces
  Underground where comes no dream;
But with living lips to cheer me,
And with ears that love to hear me?

Wilt thou take me to the shining,
  Happy, precious, fleeting past,
When the heart had no divining
  Of what liſe could be at last,
Driven out of all its courses,
Beaten back by viewless ſorces?

From the terror and the passion,
  And the loneliness and striſe,
Take me in soſt tender ſashion
  To the old sequestered life;
Let me move in the old places,
Let me look on the old ſaces.

Close against thy deep heart press me
  Till thine inmost soul I see,
With thy loveliness caress me,
  Who am tired of all but thee;
So, belovèd, till the morrow
There shall be no thought of sorrow.

CAUGHT IN THE NETS.

A.D. 1180—"This year, also, near unto Oxford in Suffolk, certain fishers took in their nets a fish, having the shape of a man in all points, which fish was kept by Bartholomew de Glandeville in the Castle of Oxford six months and more. He spake not a word; all manner of meats he did gladly eat, but most greedily raw fish. Oftentimes he was brought to the church, but never showed any sign of adoration. At length, not being well looked to, he stole to the sea, and was never seen after."—SIR RICHARD BAKER'S *Chronicle*.

"WOULD I were back, now, in my own sea caves!
Curse that March twilight, and those stormy waves
Which rioted above me till I said
I too must rise and frolic, so I sped
Up dim green twilights of the under sea;
And louder seemed the waves to call to me,
Until I dashed their foam apart, and lo!
The sky above with fire seemed to glow,
And in the waste wide glare of crimson light
Made merry the mad waves, all vast and white,
And each to each loud roared some secret thing;
And the Wind seemed a strange new song to sing,
And wantoned with the waves in violent play,
As great sea-monsters do, then fled, and they

Roared after, and made haste upon her track ;
Then, suddenly turning, she would hurl them back,
And they, with their own speed and rage made blind,
Wild, rent, and staggering before that Wind,
Fell, and in falling, dashed up high their spray,
As with it they would drown the eyes of day.

" Being of hearing quick, it seemed to me
I heard strange sounds abroad upon the sea,
That cursed March twilight ; yea, but it was fun
To swing in the waves and see the blood-red sun
Strike sharp their white and hurrying heights between,
And when the wind would cut too strong and keen,
Just for a moment the waves dive under,
And go, as it were, through the heart of the thunder.

" How sweet the weed smelt, by the wave washed
warm !
Ah, could I smell it now, and hear the storm
Make white and loud the sea above my head,
I would not leave again my soft sea bed,
And coral groves the dear sea-girls come through,
Singing the songs I love to hearken to.
That last time that I went through a great wave
Something did catch about me ; and some waif
Of monstrous floating weed it was, I thought ;

But when about my head and feet it caught
And seemed to bear me forward, surely then
I knew myself snared in the nets of men—
The nets wherein our simple fish are taken.
Then, with great fear the heart in me was shaken;
My one hope was, I knew, to break the net.
For this I strove, while, with my face down set,
Through all the interposing sea I prayed
That some bold merman would make haste to aid.
But all were in their homes—none answered me—
Only, at times, most friendly seemed the sea,
When a great wave would with a mighty blow
Send me afield; but in the fall and flow
I spun round helplessly, half choked and blind,
Hearing above the singing of the wind.
Then frantically the net I strove to rend,
But, being weak, came suddenly the end—
A strain, a rush, the wind cold on my breast,
No sea, then light—and darkness was the rest,
Until I found myself here, and breast high
In dead sea-water, and above no sky,
Nor light of sea, but something hard and black;
Ah me! if I could only once go back!

"I heard a mighty noise about me; then
I looked into the faces of cursed men.

Right hard they stared. They questioned me, I knew,
But never a word from me their cunning drew.
They gave me food, of which I was full glad,
And strange it was, and sweet, so that I had
Some joy in eating it ; and fish they gave,
Dear fish, that smelt and tasted of the wave ;
And then they left me dark and lonely there.

" There was no sound at all upon the air ;
The awful silence filled me with such dread
I violently dashed with hands and head
The water round me, that some sound might be,
Some littlest whisper from the far-off sea :
But with the light of day came sounds again,
And strange it was to me and bitter pain
To hear the wind outside, but not the sea.
Then came fresh faces and looked hard at me,
In the cold, pitiless glare of the new day.
I heard them say it was the time to pray,
And one man cast a chain my neck about,
And with a mighty grasp he dragged me out,
Right out into the sunlight and the wind,
And some men walked before, and some behind.
So on we wended, till we reached a hall,
Where all around upon their knees did fall,
And made together a most dismal noise.

Then one cried to them, in a louder voice,
Whereat more wail upon the air they poured,
Then rose. Next in their midst a monster roared,
Whereat they yelled; yea, all they yelled as one,
So that I thought by fear they were undone;
And much I marvelled that they kept their ground,
For still that monster made the dreadest sound;
Then ceased he, and they ceased, and one man rose
And shouted to them, and with many blows
Did beat himself, and long and long he screamed,
And like some fearful dream that I had dreamed
It seemed to me, and full of dread I was,
Not knowing well what next might come to pass;
But back they took me to my lonely place,
And here go by the dreary nights and days.
O shining home, wherein are all things fair,
O sea, oh world of mine, where art thou, where?
O deepsea waves, wherein strange, rare things are,
And great sea-shells, that praise the sea from far!
Green hills of slippery seaweed, wet and high,
Where green-haired mermaids love full length to lie,
Their faces in the wet weed buried deep,
Till, by their gambols tired, they fall asleep!

What joy it was to dance among the rocks
And startle, unaware, the mild sea flocks;

Or, from afar, that low, long sound to hear,
Whereby that cruel whaling-ships are near,
One whale warns all the whale-fields, and all start,
Nor rest until they reach a safer part,
To see the waves above, now green, now blue,
With light of silver fishes flashing through.

"Here through a chink I see the evening sky;
Sometimes I think my bar is not so high
But I could overleap it, and be free,
And so go forth to seek and find the sea.
Even now the gate stands open which leads out—
I hear no sound of any man about—
Shall I not do it? Gently! It is done.
Released I stand. Ah! which way shall I run?
Straight on, as well as any. Swift, my feet!
The sky is full of light, the air is sweet,
Fly fast, my feet, and faster, and more fast,
Until my long lost home be found at last.

"What sound is this ahead? O joy of joys!
It is the sea's and my own people's voice.
And as more fast I run, more loud it comes,
Mermaidens call me from their deep sea homes;
And now upon the verge of my own land
And yet within this world of men I stand.

A vast and empty place it is—ah me !
But I shall sleep to-night beneath the sea,
And wake to hear the great dear waves wash over,
And some sea-girl shall have me for her lover,
And wind about me with her cold green tresses,
And comfort me with damp and salt caresses.
Oh, world of men, good-bye, I love ye not,
Mine is a wider and a happier lot ;
White in the moonlight shines the flying foam,
Oh joy ! oh joy ! now I make haste and home."

THE BALLAD OF MONK JULIUS.

MONK JULIUS lived in a wild countrie,
And never a purer monk than he
Was vowed and wedded to chastity.

The monk was fair, and the monk was young,
His mouth seemed shaped for kisses and song,
And tender his eyes, and gentle his tongue.

He loved the Virgin, as good monks should,
And counted his beads, and kissed the rood,
But great was the pain of his manlihood.

"Sweet Mary Mother," the monk would pray,
"Take thou this curse of the flesh away—
Give me not up to the devil's sway.

"Oh, make me pure as thine own pure Son;
My thoughts are fain to be thine, each one,
But body and soul are alike undone."

And, even while praying, there came between
Himself who prayed and Heaven's own Queen
A delicate presence, more felt than seen—

The sense of woman though none was there,
Her beauty near him, her breath on the air,
Almost the touch of her hand on his hair;

And when night came, and he fell on sleep,
Warm tears in a dream his eyes would weep,
For fair, strange shapes that he might not keep—

The fair dream-girls who leaned o'er his bed,
Who held his hand, and whose kisses were shed
On his lips, for a monk's too full and red.

Oh fair dream-women, with flowing tresses
And loosened vesture! Their soft caresses
Thrilled him through to his soul's recesses.

He woke on fire, with rioting blood,
To scourge himself and to kiss the rood,
And to fear the strength of his manlihood.

One stormy night, when Christ's birth was nigh,
When snow lay thick, and the winds were high
'Twixt the large light land and the large light sky,

Monk Julius knelt in his cell's scant light,
And prayed, " If any be out to-night,
Oh Mother Mary, guide them aright."

Then there came to his ears, o'er the wastes of snow,
The dreadest of sounds, now loud, now low,
The cry of the wolves, that howl as they go.

Then followed a light, quick tap at the door ;
The monk rose up from the cell's cold floor,
And opened it, crossing himself once more.

A girl stood there, and " The wolves ! " she cried,
" No danger now, daughter," the monk replied,
And drew the beautiful woman inside,

For fair she was, as few women are fair,
Most tall and shapely ; her great gold hair
Crowned her brows, that as ivory were.

Her deep blue eyes were two homes of light,
Soft moons of beauty to his dark night—
What fairness was this to pasture sight ?

But the sight was sin, so he turned away
And knelt him down yet again to pray ;
But not one prayer could his starved lips say.

And as he knelt he became aware
Of a light hand passing across his hair,
And a sudden fragrance filled the air.

He raised his eyes, and they met her own—
How blue hers were, how they yearned and shone!
Her waist was girt with a jewelled zone,

But aside it slipped from her silken vest,
And the monk's eyes fell on her snowy breast,
Of her marvellous beauty the loveliest.

The monk sprang up, and he cried, "Oh bliss!"
His lips sought hers in a desperate kiss;
He had given his soul to make her his.

But he clasped no woman—no woman was there,
Only the laughter of fiends on the air;
The monk was snared in the devil's own snare.

RENUNCIATION.

HERE in my sheltering arms at rest she lies,
Her head upon my shoulder, and one hand
About my neck; sleep has sealed fast her eyes.
The pensive twilight gathers round the land,
The first star ventures forth into the skies,
The air is gentle, and the month is May,
And peaceful is the death of the fair day;
And with the dying day my life's hope dies—
It sinks, it sets—and then alone I stand.

How breathes she, like a little child at rest!
Above her brown hair's warmth I lean my face—
Ah me! the day when first my glad lips pressed
Her answering lips, and in a long embrace
I felt against my own her throbbing breast!
First day of love, first gathered fruit of bliss,
O day made memorable by the first kiss,
Pressure of hands, sweet secret things confessed,
Art thou not holy, day above all days?

O Love! between that first kiss and this last
How many kisses were—how sweet they were!
Still, Love, within my arms I hold you fast,
My tears and kisses fall upon your hair;
Your sleep and this brief hour will soon be past,
Then shall my heart grow strong in its endeavour,
Then shall I put you from my arms forever,
Saying, "We part, we part, and the hurricane's
blast
Sweeps over my life, and my life lies bare."

Indeed I know you thought you loved me, sweet;
You pitied me, and loved my love of you;
In all I said you heard my heart's swift beat.
"This heart that loves me so is warm and true,
A flower to wear, not trample 'neath my feet."
Thus to yourself you thought, that dear, dead day,
We sitting in the twilight still and grey,
Your hands in mine. When hands of lovers meet,
Not long, oh Love, before the lips meet, too.

Because my kisses thrilled your eager blood,
I thought I found love in your ardent kiss,
And said, "She loves!" 'Twas but your woman-
hood,
With all its great capacities for bliss.

Without a word, in time I understood,
You did not love me, though I saw you strove
To think you were returning love for love.
Oh my beloved, so passionately wooed,
In your new freedom, sweet, forget not this—

That he who loves you gives you liberty
And joy transcendent, when the rightful lover,
Predestined by mysterious powers to be
Heart of your heart, the days at length discover.
Then, fast in Love's divine captivity,
In twilights like this twilight, or some night
When earth lies still beneath the moon's large light,
Think then a little, not untenderly,
Of one who walks where only sad ghosts hover.

About my life strange winds begin to rouse—
I hear strange voices call me from afar;
Outside, the moonbeams rain through moveless boughs,
And heaven grows stronger with each confident star.
God's very peace encompasses the house;
But what have I to do with peace or Heaven?
To the outer seas let my bark be driven;
One last kiss laid on mouth and fair broad brows,
Then let me go where storm and shipwreck are.

A GREY DAY.

FORTH from a sky of windless grey
Pours down the soft, persistent rain,
And she for whom I sigh in vain,
Who makes my bliss, now makes my pain,
Being far from me this autumn day—
So far away.

Upon the waters void and grey
No floating sail appears in sight;
The dull rain and the humid light
No wind has any heart to spite,
This dreary, weary, autumn day,
With love away.

No gull wings out 'twixt grey and grey—
All grey, as far as eye can reach;
The sea too listless seems for speech,
And vaguely frets upon the beach,
As knowing she this autumn day
Is far away.

Ah, like that sea my life looks grey ;
Like a forgotten land it lies,
With no light on it from her eyes
Lovely and changeful as those skies
'Neath which she walks this autumn day
So far away.

But they shall pass, these skies of grey,
And she for whom I sigh in vain,
Who makes my bliss and makes my pain,
Shall turn my grey to gold again,
Being not, as now, that future day,
So far away.

COME, BUY.

"Some things which are not yet enrolled
In market lists are bought and sold."
—ROSSETTI'S *Jenny*.

"WHO will buy my roses—
  Roses red and white—
Sweetest of all posies
  For a man's delight?

"Who will buy my gold grass,
  Feathery, sweet, and tall—
Buy ere the summer pass,
  Sweetest thing of all?

"Who will buy my violets,
  Fresh from warm wet earth?
He who stops to buy them gets
  All his money's worth."

"I will buy your roses,
  Roses red and white,
Sweetest of all posies
  For a man's delight.

"I will buy your gold grass,
  Feathery, sweet, and tall—
Buy, ere the summer pass,
  Sweetest thing of all.

"I will buy your violets,
  Fresh from warm, wet earth,
Since he who buys them gets
  All his money's worth.

"Violets, grass, and roses,
  You are mine to-day,
When you're faded posies,
  Then I throw away."

Of Love: Eleven Lyrics.

OF LOVE: ELEVEN LYRICS.

BETWEEN JOY AND SORROW.

Between joy and sorrow,
As 'twixt day and morrow,
  I lay for a space;
And I heard, so lying,
My old Grief sighing
  From her far-off place.

I said, "Thou art over,
And where dreams hover
  Thou hoverest now;
In the land of thy dwelling
What waters are welling,
  And blossoms what bough?

"Old tears are its rivers,
The wind that there quivers
  Is breath of old sighs;

Wreck-strewn are the shores there,
And sunset endures there
   Through infinite skies.

"But all there is quiet;
There no wave makes riot
   On the waif-cumber'd coasts,
Where thou movest banished,
But not quite vanished—
   A ghost among ghosts."

IN EXTREMIS.

Now that Hope lies sick to death,
Come and weep;
None can stay her parting breath;
Dark and deep
Let her grave be—cool and quiet
Under all the summer riot.

At her head let roses be,
For a sign
Of Love's ardent wreath that she
Might not twine;
And, for Peace, she might not meet with,
Lilies cover her white feet with.

Now that she is dead and dumb,
Stay your tears;
In the years that are to come,
Sunless years,
She again will never move you,
Only hopeless sorrow prove you.

All your weeping is in vain—
        She is dead—
Her no tears can make again
        Lift her head.
Dearest, most divine deceiver,
Say your last farewell, and leave her.

AT HOPE'S GRAVE.

We said that hope was dead
  So many years ago;
We planned to make her bed
  Where all the sweet flowers blow,
To lay her quiet head
  Where the long grasses grow.

But while with tearful eyes,
  Though tears must fall in vain,
And just permitted sighs
  To ease our weary pain—
Deeming she should not rise
  Nor speak to us again—

While thus we sat, behold!
  She stirred—she was not dead;
Take off the wreath; unfold
  The shroud, raise up her head.
Not yet beneath the mould
  And flowers shall be her bed.

But now when Spring is here—
  This day, this heavy day
When skies are pure and clear,
  And earth with flowers is gay,
We clasp sad hands, my dear,
  And turn our eyes away,

Our burning eyes away,
  Because not by Hope's bed
We sit this young Spring day,
  And think that she is dead,
And find soft words to say,
  And roses for her head;

But by her very grave,
  Whereon the earth we heap,
Knowing no thing can save—
  That this *is* death, not sleep—
We stand, but do not rave,
  Too numb at heart to weep.

A BURDEN.

HAVE I not dreamed of you all night long,
Love, my Love?
Shall I not tell my dream in a song,
O my Love?

Have I not worshipped you six long years,
Queen, my Queen?
Have I not given you bounteous tears,
O my Queen?

Have I not said, when the spring was here—
"Sweet, my Sweet,
More than the pride and flower of the year,
O my sweet"?

Have I not said, in the dawning grey—
"Heart, my Heart,
I shall see my lady ere close of day,
O my Heart"?

Have I not said, in the silent night—
"Dove, my Dove,
So soft of voice and rapid of flight,
O my Dove"?

Have I not said, in the summer hours—
"Rose, my Rose,
Greatly exalted above all flowers,
O my Rose"?

Have I not said, in my great despair—
"Soul, my Soul,
Love is a grievous burden to bear
O my Soul"?

Have I not turned to the sea, and said—
"Life, my Life,
If she be not mine, be thou my bed,
O my Life"?

Have I not dreamed of your eyes, and cried—
"Light, my Light,
Lead me where love may be satisfied,
O my Light"?

Have I not trodden a weary road,
Saint, my Saint?
And where, at last, shall be my abode,
O my Saint?

Sometimes I say, in an hour supreme,
"Bride, my Bride!
I shall hold you fast, and not in a dream,
O my Bride!"

A SONG OF MEETING.

I LOOK down days and nights,
And see Love's beckoning lights
Shine from his fairest heights.

On winds that come and go
I hear, now loud, now low,
The song my heart loves so.

I know the way shall end—
The weary way I wend—
I know that God shall send

A great, propitious day,
When she I love shall say,
" Rest here, with Love to stay."

As ships to harbour bear,
Through seas and deeps of air,
Through darkness and despair,

I bring to Love's high goal,
To his supreme control,
My body and my soul.

O joy of day begun,
O joy of day just done,
Lessening the time by one,

Until her lips meet mine,
Until we drink the wine
Of Love's most hidden vine!

O in Love's land with me
Will my beloved be?
Shall our eyes live to see

Those dim and mystic ways
Haunted by many a face
Of lovers from old days?

O Love, those ways are sweet,
Their stillness so complete
We hear our own hearts beat.

And there for ever blows
Of roses, the one rose
Whose leaves for us unclose.

Love, from thy distant place,
Lift up thy loveliest face
To greet the passing days—

Each day a wave that sweeps
Back to the sunless deeps
Where Life forgotten sleeps.

O thou for whose love's sake
New souls in men might wake,
And harp of sweet song break

To know itself so slight—
Forgive Song's failing flight,
Bow, Love, from thy fair height.

FROM FAR.

"O LOVE, come back, across the weary way
Thou wentest yesterday—
Dear Love, come back!"

"I am too far upon my way to turn:
Be silent, hearts that yearn
Upon my track."

"O, Love! Love! Love! sweet Love we are undone,
If thou indeed be gone
Where lost things are."

"Beyond the extremest sea's waste light and noise,
As from Ghost-land, my voice
Is borne afar."

"O Love, what was our sin, that we should be
Forsaken thus by thee?
So hard a lot!"

"Upon your hearts my hands and lips were set—
My lips of fire—and yet,
Ye knew me not."

"Nay, surely, Love! We knew thee well, sweet Love!
Did we not breathe and move
Within thy light?"

"Ye did reject my thorns who wore my roses;
Now darkness closes
Upon your sight."

"O Love! stern Love! be not implacable.
We loved thee, Love, so well!
Come back to us."

"To whom, and where, and by what weary way
That I went yesterday,
Shall I come thus?"

"O weep, weep, weep! for Love, who tarried long
With many a kiss and song,
Has taken wing.

"No more he lightens in our eyes like fire;
He heeds not our desire,
Or songs we sing."

AFTER.

I.

A LITTLE time for laughter,
  A little time to sing,
  A little time to kiss and cling,
And no more kissing after.

II.

A little while for scheming
  Love's unperfected schemes;
  A little time for golden dreams,
Then no more any dreaming.

III.

A little while 'twas given
  To me to have thy love;
  Now, like a ghost, alone I move
About a ruined heaven.

IV.

A little time for speaking,
  Things sweet to say and hear;
  A time to seek, and find thee near,
Then no more any seeking.

V.

A little time for saying
  Words the heart breaks to say;
  A short, sharp time wherein to pray,
Then no more need for praying;

VI.

But long, long years to weep in,
  And comprehend the whole
  Great grief that desolates the soul,
And eternity to sleep in.

TOO LATE.

LOVE turns his eyes away,
  He had so long to wait
Before the words we say,
  But say, alas, too late.
He turns his eyes away.

"O, pity our dismay,
  Our sad and fallen state;
Ah, pity us, we pray,
  Let it not be too late!"
He turns his eyes away.

"O Love, up some dark way,
  If so thou wilt, and straight,
Lead us; but on some day
  Let our hands meet!" Too late.
He turns his eyes away.

"Our sky is cold and grey,
  Our life most desolate,

If we no more may lay
  Gifts on thy shrine." Too late.
He turns his eyes away.

Down drear paths we must stray,
  Each faring separate,
Because Love would not stay,
  But cried "Too late! too late!"
And turned his eyes away.

THREE SONGS.

I.

LOVE has turned his face away,
Weep, sad eyes!
Love is now of yesterday.
Time that flies,
Bringing glad and grievous things,
Bears no more Love's shining wings.

Love was not all glad, you say;
Tears and sighs
In the midst of kisses lay.
Were it wise,
If we could to bid him come,
Making with us once more home?

Little doubts that sting and prey,
Hurt replies,
Words for which a life should pay—
None denies

These of Love were very part,
Thorns that hurt the rose's heart.

Yet should we beseech Love stay,
Sorrow dies,
And if Love will but delay,
Joy may rise.
Since, with all its thorns, the rose
Is more than any flower that blows.

II.

Come in gently, and speak low,
Love lies a-dying ;
By his death-bed, standing so,
Hush, hush your crying.

Once his eyes were full of light,
Who now lies a-dying ;
Round about him falls the night,
Hush, hush your crying.

Ghostly winds begin to blow,
Love lies a-dying ;
Hark where distant waters flow,
Hush, hush your crying.

From a Land of Lost Delight—
  Now he lies a-dying—
Visions come to haunt his sight,
  Hush, hush your crying.

From a land he used to know—
  Love lies a-dying,
Ghosts of dead songs come and go,
  Hush, hush your crying.

Perished hopes like lilies white,
  Now he lies a-dying,
Leave beside him, in Death's night,
  Hush, hush your crying.

Round about him, to and fro,
  Now he lies a-dying,
Phantom feet move soft and slow,
  Hush, hush your crying.

Sharply once did sorrow bite,
  O, Love lies a-dying!
Tears and blood sprang warm and bright,
  Hush, hush your crying.

Pain is done now, strength is low,
  Love lies a-dying;
Let him gently languish so,
  Hush, hush your crying.

III.

Now we stand above Love's grave,
    Shall we weep—
We who saw and would not save?
    Let him sleep.

Shall we sing his requiem?
    Ah, for what?
Better stand here, cold and dumb;
    Vex him not.

He was young, and strong, and fair,
    Myrtle-crowned;
Now no myrtle wreathes his hair,
    Cypress bound.

Did *we* slay him? Nay, not we;
    We but said,
"Doubt and bitter words *must* be."
    He is dead!

Of those doubts and words he died.
Hush—keep still—
Late regrets would but deride.
One calm will,

Perfect peace, and perfect faith,
Had *these* been—
He had never chanced on death,
Never seen

Darkness of the under night
Where he lies,
No song on his lips, no light
In his eyes.

Leave him where he lies alone,
Void of care ;
Only carve upon his stone—
'Love *was* fair.'

Printed by WALTER SCOTT, *Felling, Newcastle-on-Tyne.*

THE SCOTT LIBRARY—continued.

English Prose.
The Pillars of Society.
Fairy and Folk Tales.
Essays of Dr. Johnson.
Essays of Wm. Hazlitt.
Landor's Pentameron, &c.
Poe's Tales and Essays.
Vicar of Wakefield.
Political Orations.
Holmes's Autocrat.
Holmes's Poet.
Holmes's Professor.
Chesterfield's Letters.
Stories from Carleton.
Jane Eyre.
Elizabethan England.
Davis's Writings.
Spence's Anecdotes.
More's Utopia.
Sadi's Gulistan.
English Folk Tales.
Northern Studies.
Famous Reviews.
Aristotle's Ethics.
Landor's Aspasia.
Tacitus.
Essays of Elia.
Balzac.
De Musset's Comedies.
Darwin's Coral-Reefs.
Sheridan's Plays.
Our Village.
Humphrey's Clock, &c.
Tales from Wonderland.
Douglas Jerrold.
Rights of Woman.
Athenian Oracle.
Essays of Sainte-Beuve.
Selections from Plato.
Heine's Travel Sketches.
Maid of Orleans.
Sydney Smith.
The New Spirit.
Marvellous Adventures.
(From the Morte d'Arthur.)
Helps's Essays.
Montaigne's Essays.
Luck of Barry Lyndon.
William Tell.
Carlyle's German Essays.
Lamb's Essays.
Wordsworth's Prose.
Leopardi's Dialogues.
Inspector-General (Gogol)
Bacon's Essays.
Prose of Milton.

www.ingramcontent.com/pod-product-compliance
Lightning Source LLC
Chambersburg PA
CBHW030857270326
41929CB00008B/454
* 9 7 8 3 7 4 4 7 1 2 3 1 6 *